ISAAC COLLINS

A Quaker Printer
in 18th Century America

ISAAC
COLLINS

A Quaker Printer
in 18th Century America

Richard F. Hixson

RUTGERS UNIVERSITY PRESS

New Brunswick, New Jersey

To the memory of my father
Frederick Grant Hixson

PREFACE

The career of Isaac Collins constitutes an important part of the early history of printing, publishing, and journalism in the Middle States. From his presses in Philadelphia, Burlington and Trenton, New Jersey, and New York City, in the years 1770 to 1808, came some of the finest specimens of American printing. He was foremost a book publisher and bookseller, but he also published a Revolutionary newspaper and served as New Jersey's official government printer.

Collins issued many Quaker tracts and histories as well as numerous books about other faiths; however, he was equally well known as the publisher of outstanding works on slavery, education, American history, and medicine. His greatest single achievement as publisher and craftsman was his 1791 edition of the King James Bible, the second quarto edition to be printed in America. To this work Collins brought all the skills of an eminent master printer and typographer, but in his solid concern for a definitive text he enlisted the aid not only of Friends but of prominent Episcopalians, Baptists, and Presbyterians, including Dr. John Witherspoon of Princeton. The Collins Bible still commands the admiration of scholars and fine printers.

As founding publisher and editor for more than eight years of the *New-Jersey Gazette,* New Jersey's first established newspaper, Collins persisted in concepts of freedom of the press that sometimes conflicted with those of traditionalist legislators and politicians. Ironically, in his wholehearted support of the patriot cause during the Revolution, Collins was subject to the attacks of extremists who, in the words of Arthur M. Schlesinger, believed that "liberty of speech belonged solely to those who spoke the speech of liberty." Collins's position was simple: "My ear is open to every Man's Instruction but to no Man's influences."

In addition to his regular business of publishing a variety of books, pamphlets, almanacs, and broadsides, typical imprints of his time, Collins held the coveted position of public printer, first to the colony and then to the new state. Few men in the printing trade were so well placed to observe at firsthand the ideological development of the new nation. As John Adams wrote to Thomas Jefferson, legislative records, pamphlets, and newspapers ought to be consulted for those years "to ascertain the steps by which the public opinion was enlightened and informed."

Devout Quaker though he was, Collins held strong personal ideals of public justice and self-defense that in wartime ran counter to the precepts of the Society of Friends. He was disowned by the Quakers for nearly a decade on the grounds that his services as official printer to a revolutionary government and publisher of a patriot newspaper were tantamount to service in the militia and hence inconsistent with the Friends's peaceable testimony. On the slavery issue, however, he had the full approval of his brethren, for he early freed his own slave and then helped in the movement to forbid slaveholding generally by welcoming manuscripts by reformers at a time when other printers did not.

Collins's place in the eighteenth-century scene has been somewhat obscured by the shadow of more vocal and more versatile contemporaries, as well as by human predilections for the spectacular and the unusual. But it is my belief that if we are to know the full history of printing and publishing in the United States, and the significance of these activities in our culture, we must first study the life and times of the people who laid down early patterns and standards. Men like Collins, working quietly but effectively, dedicated to their professions, made lasting contributions to the progress of the new nation.

In the preparation of this biography I have depended on the advice and research assistance of many persons and institutions.

I had the great pleasure of meeting and corresponding with several of Isaac Collins's descendants, notably Grellet N. Collins and Marian T. Grieb of Chestertown, Maryland, and Mrs. Dorr Viele of Cambridge, Massachusetts. The John Wesley Jarvis oil of Isaac Collins has come down to Grellet Collins, and it is with his kind permission that the portrait is reproduced in this book. Mrs. Grieb showed me an assortment of family items. These fine people offered me all their help.

Next I wish to thank my colleagues in the Rutgers University School of Journalism, especially its director, Professor Frederic E. Merwin, for their encouragement and concern at every stage of my work. I am also grateful to the university's Research Council for financial support.

I am much indebted to the many librarians who acquainted me with their collections and bore with my questions, especially Donald A. Sinclair, Anthony S. Nicolosi, and Irene K. Lionikis of the Special Collections Department of the Rutgers library. Without their confidence and genuine interest this biography could not have been completed.

Among the other librarians and curators who were helpful were Marjorie F. Davis, Haverford College; Dorothy G. Harris, Swarthmore College; Marcus A. McCorison and Louise S. Marshall, American Antiquarian Society; Catherine Miller and John D. Kilbourne, Historical Society of Pennsylvania; Rebecca B. Muehleck, Trenton Free Public Library; Mary Ogilvie, Philadelphia Yearly Meeting of Friends; Vincent Rourke, Burlington County Historical Society; Carolyn Scoon, New York Historical Society; Glen R. Skillin, Brown University; Murphy Smith, American Philosophical Society; Edmund A. Stanley, Jr., Bowne & Co., New York City; Harold W. Thompson, Jr., and Magdalena Houlroyd, Glassboro State College; and Lillian Tonkin, Library Company of Philadelphia.

In addition, I owe a great deal to several friends and colleagues. Professor Lyon N. Richardson has long encouraged my interest in early American history, and it was Professor Merwin who reminded me of the deficiencies in our knowledge of New Jersey printing history and suggested the present study. Willman Spawn of the Amercan Philosophical Society and his wife, Carol, advised me on many difficult problems of research on eighteenth-century printing. I benefited greatly from the comments of Paul S. Dunkin, who read the manuscript at an early stage. George C. Rockefeller also offered suggestions on the manuscript, besides allowing me the use of his personal collection of books and documents.

My typists were Janet Riordan, Barbara Hye, Karen Gyurecz, and Beverly Piano, and I herewith express my appreciation to them.

The extent of my family's contribution is immeasurable. For their patience and understanding I thank my wife, Cynthia, and our children, Todd and Nancy.

RICHARD F. HIXSON

Middlebush, New Jersey
September, 1967

CONTENTS

ISAAC COLLINS

*A Quaker Printer
in 18th Century America*

⋖ I ⋗

APPRENTICE

Isaac Collins was born near Centerville, Delaware, on February 16, 1746. His father, Charles, had quit his trade as a wine cooper in Bristol, England, to seek a new life as a farmer in America. A Quaker from a "veritable hotbed of Quakerism,"[1] Charles Collins, aged nineteen and an orphan, left England in 1734 on one of the frequent sailings for the American colonies. His ship was probably bound for Philadelphia, but he debarked at the first port of entry on the Delaware River—New Castle, Delaware, a town heavily populated by Quakers.

Besides the wealth from their rich farmlands, Delaware inhabitants enjoyed a considerable degree of self-government and personal liberty, factors undoubtedly attractive to Charles Collins. The colony, made up of three counties that once were part of Pennsylvania, possessed an ideal climate and a fertile soil owing to its eastern exposure on Delaware Bay and the Atlantic Ocean. After working as a hired hand to earn enough to buy his own farm, Charles Collins selected a small place near Centerville in Brandywine Hundred, an old political subdivision in the northern part of New Castle County near the Pennsylvania border.

He married Miss Sarah Hammond of nearby Chester County, Pennsylvania (the date is not certain), and she eventually bore him two children, Elizabeth and Isaac. Of Elizabeth's life we know nothing except that she never married; however, Isaac's mention of her in his will suggests a relationship that must have been amicable if not close over the years.

In Brandywine Hundred, education and religion, as well as farming, were important concerns. Isaac probably learned his letters at home, the small Center Meeting House in Centerville, and the Friends' school in Wilmington. If the Collinses followed the customs of their sect, they must have spent a great amount of their leisure time among other Friends, particularly at meeting on First Day.

Typical meeting houses were furnished with plain wooden benches, and a frame partition divided the men and boys from the women and girls. The basis of the Collinses' Quaker faith was inward inspiration; the Friends' religious discipline taught them the values of plain living and the meaning of the "totality of souls united with God," the invisible church. The Quaker way of life required of its members total commitment to what Friends called the "Inner Light." [2]

A farmer's son in those days was expected to help his

father look after the livestock and tend the crops of rye, barley, corn, and assorted fruits and vegetables for the table. At harvest time they hauled the grain to one of the many mills that dotted the path of the rocky, swift Brandywine Creek. The establishment of gristmills on Delaware's several creeks was, according to one historian, "as important to the history of Delaware as the Revolution of 1776." [3]

In the wintertime, when there were fewer outdoor chores, the children could sometimes attend classes at the log schoolhouse on the meeting house grounds and play on the banks of the Brandywine, an exciting if dangerous pastime. At the end of the day Isaac and Elizabeth may have listened to their father read, perhaps from religious tracts. Common among the books and pamphlets printed in England and shipped to the colonies were the Bible and the writings of Robert Barclay, William Penn, and Isaac Pennington. In years to come, Isaac would himself publish the works of some famous Quaker authors.

The year 1760 brought sudden and significant changes in Isaac's life. On his mother's death sometime earlier, his father had married again. Now on his father's death and his stepmother's remarriage and removal from the neighborhood, Isaac became the ward of his mother's brother, John Hammond, who resided in Wilmington. His father's second marriage had yielded two more children, William, who died in youth, and Sarah, about whom little is known. Sarah's children, whose surname was McQuire, are mentioned in Isaac's will; thus he must have had some interest in the family tie. As to how many of the children besides Isaac John Hammond took as his wards, the record is again unclear. Isaac lost touch with his stepmother after his father's death, for he makes this point some fourteen years later in a letter inquiring about his family background.[4]

Another event that altered Isaac's life not long after the death of his father was his indenture as an apprentice. His master, the printer James Adams, had spent several years with the firm of Franklin and Hall in Philadelphia, beginning in 1753, and set up his own shop in the same city about a year before he moved to Wilmington to avoid competition. Adams's arrival in town marked the beginning of the printing industry in Delaware, which had previously depended upon Philadelphia craftsmen for its printing needs. Adams announced the opening of his new shop in the *Pennsylvania Gazette* for September 24, 1761, and promised to "undertake and execute all printing work committed to his care." He stocked his bookstore, a traditional part of the colonial printing office, with "Bibles, Testaments, spelling-books, and primmers, all sorts of blanks, viz. bills of lading, bonds with and without judgment, penal bills, bills of sale, apprentices indentures, powers of attorneys, wills and powers, and arbitration bonds." Adams's assortment was typical.

Apprenticeships in eighteenth-century America served not only to alleviate the problems of rearing large families and introducing young people to the crafts in their communities but also to supply cheap labor for the various trades and professions. In the printing trade the apprentice was often the master printer's despair. The assignments were difficult and menial, allowing for few hours away from the job, and it was not uncommon for the youngsters to run away frequently. Most of the time they were apprehended and returned to their masters;

some, however, were never heard from again. Printers regularly advertised for new apprentices to replace those who had either run away or finished their indentures.

Young Collins's apprenticeship with Adams must have been like those of the scores of lads who augmented the labor force in printing. He would have vowed, for example, to serve faithfully his master and mistress. "Their secrets he shall keep close; their commandments honest and lawful everywhere he shall gladly obey; he shall do no damage to his said master, &c. nor suffer it to be done by others without letting or giving seasonable notice thereof to his said master; he shall not waste the goods of his said master, &c. nor lend them unlawfully to any." Further, the apprentice pledged to stay away from cards, dice, taverns, and alehouses. His indenture forbade him to marry during the term of the contract. For their part, the master and his family were obligated to provide the apprentice with room, board, and clothing. They were to oversee his instruction in reading, writing, arithmetic, and the printing trade.[5]

One of Isaac's important early jobs as an apprentice, in addition to cleaning up after the printer, was that of "beating," a step preparatory to making the printed impressions on the press. He first spread thick ink on a mixing block, or stone, and with two stuffed leather-covered balls attached to handles he collected the substance and transferred it to the type the printer had set in composition. Then, by carefully rolling the balls back and forth, he spread the ink evenly and thinly over the surface of the type. After each impression the process began anew, the "beater" inking the type and the "puller," or pressman, closing and opening the press. Two experienced pressmen, working at top speed, could produce upwards of 240 printed sheets an hour.[6]

Besides carrying out his many shop assignments, Collins was often called upon to help his mistress with culinary and other household chores. Sometimes these duties conflicted, and it was up to the master and the mistress to solve the problem. Isaiah Thomas, the famous Massachusetts printer, related in his history of printing how on one occasion a pressman in Adams's shop, whose pay depended on the amount of work he produced, discovered an ingenious way to overcome the delay in his presswork. When the boy was called away to the kitchen, the pressman continued to pull the sheets as usual, leaving enough time between each sheet for the form of type to be reinked. Adams, upon inspecting the piles of printed sheets and perceiving so many faintly printed copies, asked the pressman the meaning of the poor quality. "I suppose the boy has not beat them," replied the pressman, "but I am sure I leave him time enough and have also performed my duty in pulling." Though Adams was diverted by the humor of the situation, he ordered the apprentice never again to leave his post.[7]

A colonial printer who sought to make his shop an indispensable part of the community, as most of them did, issued an almanac, and each printer tried to make his as different as possible from the scores of others. Thus, among the items Adams printed in the fall of 1761 was the *Wilmington Almanack for 1762*. In addition to the standard astrological and ecclesiastical data, it contained "select" pieces on such subjects as matrimony and happiness. From the start, therefore, Collins learned of the intricate details involved in producing the most popular commodity of the colonial shop. As a master printer some years later, he too would seek public attention with an almanac.

Another Adams imprint during Collins's first year as an apprentice was the popular *Child's New Spelling-Book,* a slight, paper-bound volume designed "to enlarge children's ideas, and give them an early sense of the infinite obligations they lie under to the great Author of their beings." Also from the shop that year came at least one broadside, *Advice of Evan Ellis to His Daughter When at Sea,* and a ready reckoner, *Merchant's and Trader's Security,* which contained financial tables and other useful commercial information.[8]

Dorothy Lawson Hawkins, a bibliographer of Adams imprints, is convinced that Adams issued four imprints between September 24, the day he announced his move to Wilmington, and November 5, 1761, when his first newspaper advertisement appeared; however, the almanac and the broadside are the only two extant.[9]

Adams's major work in 1762 was the first book printed in Delaware, Thomas Dilworth's *A New Guide to the English Tongue,* a reprint of a popular English grammar. It contained more than 140 pages and was one of the most ambitious jobs for the Adams shop during Collins's apprenticeship there. In later years Collins himself published some of Dilworth's works.

Gradually, as the number and variety of imprints from the Wilmington shop increased, Adams's ward and printing assistant was further acquainted with the scope of his craft and with the typical products of the country's infant printing industry. To cite an example, the little shop issued in 1763 a government-sponsored compilation of

Delaware laws. Such volumes were given high priority in printing shops, for they served to defray routine maintenance costs. The extent to which colonial governments, in turn, depended upon the printing shops to publish their laws and proclamations can be measured by the great number of shops that were set up expressly for the purpose of publishing government documents.

What may have furnished an introduction to journalism for Collins was Adams's plan to publish a newspaper. Few colonial printers failed to attempt such publications, for by Adams's time newspapers had become the principal means for creative printers to express themselves and eighteenth-century American printers delighted in distributing their weekly journals among townspeople and farm dwellers. The *Wilmington Courant,* according to Isaiah Thomas, made its appearance "about the year 1762." Thomas states that it lasted for about six months, when, "for want of encouragement," it disappeared.[10] Later printing historians doubt the existence of the *Courant,* even for this short period, since no copies are extant. But whether Adams actually published a newspaper or merely announced his proposal for printing one, the fact is that Collins, as a member of the printer's household, must have overheard conversations about this rather new means of communication in the colonies.

Collins stayed with Adams for about five years, or until early in 1766. How many fellow apprentices Collins met during that time it is impossible to know exactly. Printers seldom needed more than one or two apprentices and, in Adams's case, his three sons eventually became journeymen under his tutelage. It was during this period, no doubt, that Collins first met Shepard Kollock, who also served his apprenticeship with Adams. Kollock, a native of Lewes, Delaware, site of the colony's first settlement, later went on, like Collins, to work for William Goddard in Philadelphia. Also like Collins, he eventually became a newspaper publisher in New Jersey. Their friendship lasted many years.

A slowdown in business in 1766 forced Adams to release Collins, then twenty years old, to complete the last year of his apprenticeship elsewhere. He went to Virginia to work for William Rind, a fiery Whig printer who had been brought from Annapolis to Williamsburg to start the second *Virginia Gazette*. Since newspaper publishing became an important part of Collins's career, we may assume that he was attracted to Rind's shop by the prospect of learning more about this aspect of his trade.

Williamsburg in the eighteenth century was more than the seat of the colony's government; it was Virginia's center of religion, education, commerce, and social fashion. Some travelers viewed it as a small English country town; others believed it to be a boiling metropolis in the new world. An anonymous Frenchman who visited the town in 1765, the year before Collins took up residence there, described how it shed its normal placid appearance when the courts and the General Assembly were in session. "In the Day time people hurying back and forwards from the Capitoll to the taverns, and at night, Carousing and Drinking In one Chamber and box and Dice in another, which Continues till morning Commonly." [11] On the other hand, a teacher at the College of William and Mary, writing several years earlier, said: "Here dwell several very good families, and more reside here in their own houses at publick times. They live in the same neat manner, dress after the same modes, and behave themselves exactly as the gentry in London; most families of any note having a coach, chariot, berlin, or chaise." [12]

Of importance for Collins when he arrived in town to take his first job on a newspaper, Williamsburg was still ringing with Patrick Henry's denunciation in 1765 of the Stamp Act. Newspaper printers generally abhorred the new British law because it taxed the paper they used. The statute also called for the asessment of two shillings for each advertisement, which amounted to a real hardship since the publishers earned but three to five shillings for the first insertion, less for repeated ones. Job printing was hurt, too, for printers had to pay a tax on pamphlets, almanacs, and legal and business forms. Moreover, the new law levied a toll on apprenticeship indentures, thereby hitting the printing trade's basic source of labor. Yet, despite these economic handicaps, the Stamp Act proved politically advantageous—"fortunate for the liberties of America," as a contemporary historian put it. [13]

The first press to be established in Williamsburg was that of William Parks, who set up shop in the colony in 1730. In 1732 he was appointed to the enviable position of Virginia's first government printer. He established the first *Virginia Gazette* in 1736 and continued its publication until his death in 1750. Parks was succeeded both as government printer and as newspaper publisher by one of his journeymen, William Hunter, who owned the business until his death eleven years later. Hunter's brother-in-law, Joseph Royle, then assumed control but only for five years. When Royle died in 1766, Alexander Purdie and John Dixon took over the business.

Until the arrival of competition in the person of Rind

sometime early in 1766, the Williamsburg press had been entirely controlled by these Royalist printers; despite their claims of nonpartisanship, they were reluctant to risk estrangement from the ruling government, which, after all, held the purse strings on public printing. Of Rind's coming, Thomas Jefferson recalled years later: "We had but one press, and that having the whole business of the government, and no competitor for public favor, nothing disagreeable to the governor could be got into it. We procured Rind to come from Maryland to publish a free paper." [14]

It is possible that Collins read or heard about Rind's notice of May 9, 1766, in Purdie and Dixon's *Virginia Gazette*. The town's new printer announced his intentions to engage in the printing business and to begin publication of another newspaper the following week; and he aligned himself with those colonists who were dissatisfied with British rule. Meanwhile, Purdie and Dixon, "Tired with an involuntary recess from business" due to the financial hardships imposed by the Stamp Act, began issuing their own *Gazette* unstamped on March 7. This was an effort to curry favor with the Whigs, with the added assurances that their *Gazette* would "be as free as any Gentleman can wish, or desire." Despite these words of compliance the printers did not enjoy the Whigs' complete confidence. Consequently, in Governor Francis Fauquier's words, "some of the hot Burgesses" got Rind to undertake a rival publication with the promise of legislative printing. [15]

During Collins's brief tenure with him (just long enough to finish his apprenticeship), Rind devoted a large measure of his effort to the *Gazette*, "Open to ALL

PARTIES, but influenced by NONE." Soon, as promised by Jefferson and his followers, he was assigned by the House of Burgesses to be the official Virginia government printer over Purdie, the governor's favorite candidate. Collins, therefore, assisted in the printing of government laws, as he had with Adams, and in the weekly composition of a newspaper. He also helped print an almanac.

In the process of learning his trade, Collins improved his ability to set type in a composing stick, transfer the type to a galley, and place the assembled composition onto the surface of an imposing stone. He increased his speed in picking out letters and numerals accurately from the big wooden type cases and returning them quickly after the job was completed. Speed was essential because printing shops owned small supplies of type and almost always the type that was set for one portion of a job had to be used for another part of the same job.

On his twenty-first birthday, February 16, 1767, Collins's apprenticeship was over, and the young man left Rind to seek his first employment as a journeyman printer in Philadelphia, the printing and publishing capital of the colonies.

William Penn's "green country town" had grown by 1767 to approximately 30,000 inhabitants, to become the largest of all the colonial cities. Industrially stable and rich in cultural variety, Philadelphia was a proud town, proud of its size, proud of its heritage, and proud of its extensive trade with Great Britain and the West Indies. To a young man, Philadelphia's size, its tremendous wealth and influence, must have appeared awesome. At first, no doubt, Collins was bewildered by the seemingly countless mercantile houses, with their brick fronts and tiny window panes, the different signs swinging gently, the iron balconies, the uncomplicated cornices, and the moderately pitched roofs, with lines interrupted only once or twice by a dormer; one could easily divert himself by trying to count the chimney pots.[16]

Like Boston and New York, Philadelphia was a center of intellectual activity. It was the home of Benjamin Franklin, founder of the American Philosophical Society, father of the University of Pennsylvania, and, most important to Collins, printer and newspaper publisher. Other prominent Philadelphians distinguished in science, art, and letters were Dr. Benjamin Rush, David Rittenhouse, Charles Wilson Peale, and John Dickinson. Among the town's leading Quakers were the Pembertons and Logans, John Bartram, the botanist, Thomas Godfrey, the inventor, and Benjamin West, the painter. To this impressive list may be added the name of William Goddard, an ambitious printer who had left Providence in 1766 to create a Philadelphia newspaper on the grandest scale ever before attempted in the colonies.

Then but twenty-six, Goddard had already made his mark by becoming the first government printer in Providence and publisher of that city's first newspaper, the *Gazette*. As a leading proponent of independence, Goddard was responsible for the first printed newspaper in New Jersey, a one-issue attack on the Stamp Act. In Philadelphia, however, he established a secret partnership with Joseph Galloway, speaker of the Pennsylvania Assembly, and Thomas Wharton, a wealthy Quaker merchant. They issued the first number of the *Pennsylvania Chronicle* on January 26, 1767, while Goddard's mother and sister stayed on in Providence to manage his *Gazette*.

The *Chronicle* was the best-looking newspaper yet produced in Philadelphia, and perhaps in any of the colonies. It had a cleaner appearance than either of the other Philadelphia papers, Franklin's *Gazette*, edited since 1766 by David Hall, and William Bradford's *Journal*. The *Chronicle*'s pages were folio size, with four columns instead of the customary three, a feature that supposedly cost Goddard an additional £200 a year for paper. It was patterned after the *London Chronicle*, and, interestingly, Goddard numbered the pages consecutively from issue to issue, indicating that the young publisher was confident his readers would want to compile their own annual volumes.[17]

Early in February 1767 Goddard advertised for a journeyman printer and an apprentice. Three months later he sought another printer. Collins may have answered one of these advertisements; however, another new hand who started about this time was Shepard Kollock, Goddard's nephew. Benjamin Mecom, a nephew of Franklin's, also worked for Goddard on several occasions and later served Collins in New Jersey. The printing office prospered, supported mainly by the *Chronicle*, which within three months had the second largest circulation in the colonies. New Jersey, which did not have its own newspaper, was second to Pennsylvania in the number of subscribers. By 1770 the circulation climbed to 2,500 for all thirteen colonies, the West Indies, Canada, and London.

The years Collins lived in Philadelphia—from the spring of 1767 until the summer of 1770—were decisive ones for the colonies. With the passage of the Townshend Act in 1767, opposition to British control and excessive taxation flared up as it had in the days following the Stamp Act. It is not surprising, therefore, to find the *Chronicle* the first newspaper to publish the *Letters from a Pennsylvania Farmer,* a series of twelve essays by John Dickinson against the right of Parliament to tax the colonies in any form. So popular were the letters that Hall and Bradford immediately clipped them and began running the series in their own papers. But they were so inflammatory that their publication in the *Chronicle* marked the beginning of the end of Goddard's partnership with Galloway and Wharton because his backers favored the continuation of British rule. If Collins witnessed the altercation among the partners, it probably represented his first personal experience with the conflict inherent in newspaper publishing. To publish a newspaper, Collins eventually came to realize, was tantamount to inviting harassment from some quarter.

Another public controversy reported and debated in the Philadelphia press concerned the building of a theater just outside the city. The early Christian fathers had considered theatrical performances "corrupting to morals and an impediment to salvation," opined a writer in the *Gazette* for February 5, 1767. "Philadelphus," writing in the *Chronicle,* denounced the drama for its "blasphemous speeches, wanton amours, profane jests and impure passions." An actor defended the theater in a later number of the *Gazette* and accused the other writers of a "torrent of incomprehensible abuse." Newspapers of Collins's time truly were community platforms. Rhetorical battles raged frequently, and editors were seldom without controversial issues; especially welcome were issues which both performed a public service and increased readership.

From Goddard's shop Collins learned more about the idiosyncrasies of the printing business than he had from either Adams or Rind. For one thing, the competition in Philadelphia meant that in order to be a successful printer one's imprints had to be superior. There were mediocre craftsmen, to be sure, but Collins seems never to have settled for minimal standards. Collins's first master, Adams, has been called "a printer who possessed real craftsmanship, and his work may be compared without discredit with that of the best American printers of his time." [18] According to Ward Miner, Goddard was "one of the outstanding printers in eighteenth century America." [19]

The year 1770 opened with Collins's acceptance into the membership of the Philadelphia Monthly Meeting and the formation of his business partnership with Joseph Crukshank. The minutes of the meeting for December 29, 1769, include this brief item: "Isaac Collins, a sound young man of sober conduct who has for some years past attended our meetings for worship, now requests to be joined in membership with us." His request was granted officially on January 26.[20] Crukshank, whom Collins had met through their mutual religious background, was a native Philadelphian who had been an apprentice to Andrew Stewart. In 1769 he had gone into business for himself on Second Street near Chestnut.

The partnership lasted less than a year, from January until August, but it marked the start of a friendship that continued for many years. The new firm continued to operate from Crukshank's address for a short while before moving to larger quarters on Third Street "opposite the Work-House." The young journeymen issued seven imprints, and since these were the first to bear Collins's name, they are worth brief examination. The partners' first imprint was a private job for Dr. John Kearsley, Jr., a sixteen-page pamphlet entitled *A Narrative of Many Facts, Relating to the Late Disputed Will of Samuel Flower*. Soon after completing the job the printers moved into their quarters on Third Street.[21]

The next imprint, which turned out to be historically if not financially important, was the first volume in a proposed set of twelve, entitled *Materials Towards a History of the American Baptists in Pennsylvania*, by the Rev. Morgan Edwards of Philadelphia. The second volume was not issued until 1792, and by another printer, Thomas Dobson. The volume printed by Collins and Crukshank is valued today as the first historical work written and printed in Pennsylvania. Of more immediate practical use was a thirty-two-page book, *Directions for the Breeding and Management of Silk-Worms*, consisting of extracts from the writings of experts François Bossier de Sauvages and Samuel Pullen (or Pullien).

The printers had been requested to publish this handbook by Dr. Cadwalader Evans, who, as a member of the American Philosophical Society, had received a copy of the Frenchman's original treatises from Benjamin Franklin in London. Another member of the society, the Rev. Jonathan Odell, rector of St. Mary's Episcopal Church in Burlington, New Jersey, did the translation. Pullen's comments, printed as part of the appendix, were included, Rev. Odell said in the preface, "to further elucidate the French treatises."

The silk industry flourished in eastern Pennsylvania before and after the Revolution. Cocoons, spun as far away as Bethlehem, were brought by the thousands to Philadelphia, where a filature had been established to reel the silk. Farmers and city dwellers alike went into the business of raising mulberry trees and selling silk-worm eggs. Therefore, with the publication of a breeders' handbook, the young printers contributed to the advancement of silk manufacturing in America. Besides being of practical use, the book reviewed the rise and progress of the "Scheme for Encouraging the Culture of Silk" in Pennsylvania and adjacent colonies.

Typical of the output of the colonial printer were the countless pamphlets on political and religious topics. Among the favorite authors were Dryden, Swift, Johnson, Pope, Addison, Steele, and Milton. Their works were widely reprinted and eagerly read. To this category Collins and Crukshank contributed the first American edition of Milton's *Considerations Touching the Likeliest Means to Remove Hirelings Out of the Church,* first published in England in 1659. They did the printing for Robert Bell, a recent immigrant from Scotland who in three short years had acquired a reputation as Philadelphia's most popular bookseller and auctioneer. Bell was also responsible for the first American editions of Milton's great poetic dramas *Paradise Lost, Paradise Regained,* and *Samson Agonistes.*

Alexander Cluny's *The American Traveller,* another Collins and Crukshank imprint during 1770, examined a number of the advantages of the colonies' continued union with Great Britain, and thereby contributed to the debate between those persons who were for separation and those who were against it. The printers inserted a notice opposite the table of contents stating that the present state of

affairs between England and her American colonies justi-
fied publication of the book. "Mutual Advantage is the
most solid Basis, the strongest Cement of Union, in all
Connections, whether political or private. To shew such
Advantage . . . must be the most effectual Means of
preserving that Union, so much and so wisely wished for,
by every Friend of his Country."

Cluny, in his own words an "old and Experienced
Trader," had compiled *The American Traveller* over a
period of thirty years and, in a series of letters written
originally to an English earl, had set down his observations "on the present state, culture and commerce of the
British colonies in America, and the further improvements
of which they are capable." He accounted for the exports
and imports of each colony, together with the amount of
revenue accruing to Great Britain. The book met with
immediate public acceptance, as evidenced by its mention
in numerous bookstore advertisements. Equally popular
were two imprints issued by Collins and Crukshank, Mary
Collyer's translation of *The Death of Abel* by the Swiss
poet Solomon Gessner and *An Account of the Convincement, Exercises, Services and Travels of Richard Davies,*
the only work by the Welsh Quaker.

Reprinting of old favorites was a common practice in
the early days of America's own literary development.
Gessner's book was first printed in this country in 1762
by William Bradford in Philadelphia and by the Boston
firm of Fowle and Draper. Hugh Gaine, of New York,
brought out two more editions in 1765 and 1766. Davies'
book was first printed in London in 1710, two years after
the author's death. A Philadelphia printer, James Chat-
tin, published the second edition in 1752. Collins and

Crukshank issued the eighth edition of Gessner and the third of Davies.

Collins's brief partnership with Crukshank appears to have been profitable for both men, particularly in terms of experience. Yet Collins would not enjoy the complete freedom and responsibility of a so-called master printer until he had engaged in business wholly for himself and had in this capacity employed other craftsmen.

In the nine-year period which had begun in 1761 in Wilmington and had led to Philadelphia, Collins worked diligently to learn the skills necessary for the years ahead. From his teachers—who were among the finest available—he also acquired the habits of industry and frugality in business. From the strong Quaker sense of orderliness he learned the values of prudence and honesty in business. "Quakers are accustomed from childhood to apply order to the distribution of their tasks, their thoughts, and every moment of their lives," observed a French visitor to Philadelphia. "They carry this spirit of order everywhere; it economizes time, activity and money." [22]

◄§ II §►

MASTER
PRINTER

In 1770, after several exploratory business visits to Burlington, New Jersey, which had no resident printer, Collins decided to open a shop there.

The second oldest Quaker colony in the province of West Jersey, Burlington had been settled in 1677, before William Penn's first colonists arrived in Philadelphia, and had gained prominence as the capital of the province and as an official port of entry. After 1702, when West and East Jersey became a single province, it was one of the two seats of government of the colonial legislature, the other being Perth Amboy in East Jersey.

In many ways Burlington was more a part of Pennsylvania and the Delaware Valley than of New Jersey. Then, as now, the inhabitants of East Jersey had an affinity with New York, and those of West Jersey maintained close ties with Philadelphia. "New York and Philadelphia are in Reality the Commercial Capitals of East and West Jersey," said William Franklin, New Jersey's last royal governor.[1] The Friends' Yearly Meeting, the policy-making body of the Quakers in the Middle Colonies, which had from 1686 until 1761 convened alternately in Philadelphia and Burlington, was in Collins's time conducted in the larger city. Though Collins lived and worked in Burlington, he remained a citizen of greater Philadelphia.

During his preliminary visits to Burlington, Collins had met members of the influential Smith family at their imposing home at the corner of High and Broad Streets, the center of town politically as well as geographically. Collins had known of John Smith, the prominent Burlington Quaker who became a member of the governor's Council and a powerful New Jersey legislator, as an early subscriber and frequent literary contributor to William Goddard's *Chronicle*. Using the name of "Atticus," Smith wrote about seventy nonpolitical essays which appeared in the newspaper from February 1767 through August 1770.

It is no exaggeration to say that the Smith family, known as "liberal" Quakers, controlled much of the religious and political life of the town and West Jersey in the eighteenth century. Their influence extended well beyond the Society of Friends and the city of Burlington into the colony's legislative chambers.

John Smith's father, Richard, had served the city of Burlington from 1730 until 1748 and was, according to an Anglican clergyman, "the head of the Quaquors [sic]" in the New Jersey Assembly.[2] John Smith's two brothers, Samuel, the historian, and Richard, a rising young political figure, also had a place in the history of New Jersey.

Richard later attended the first Continental Congress; Samuel became a member of the Assembly in 1754 and gained a Council seat in 1763.

Samuel Smith is best known today for his *History of the Colony of Nova-Caesaria, or New Jersey,* which was published in Woodbridge, New Jersey, in 1765, by James Parker, official public printer of New Jersey from 1758 until his death in 1770.

The tradition of public printing in New Jersey had begun in 1723, the year William Bradford of New York issued a volume of Assembly laws, recorded as the first New Jersey imprint. Bradford had taken a press from New York to Perth Amboy to print paper currency for the province and, while there, also printed the laws. Bradford and his son Andrew conducted the public printing for New Jersey until 1728, at which time Samuel Keimer of Philadelphia began to carry out government printing assignments in Burlington. Benjamin Franklin, then employed occasionally by Keimer, had printed issues of currency in the same shop Collins was to occupy in 1770. Parker, who had learned the printing trade from the elder Bradford, established the first "permanent" press in New Jersey in 1751. Three years later he began to receive a share of the government printing, and in 1758 became the province's official public printer.

Outside experts such as printers were frequently called upon by New Jersey legislators, as illustrated by an episode involving Franklin. He returned to Burlington in 1736 to print more money for the colony and was implored two years later to help the Assembly in drawing up an answer to one of Governor Lewis Morris's controversial messages to the lower house. An unyielding and unpopular executive, Morris seldom enjoyed good relations with the legislators during his governorship, which began in 1738 and ended with his death in 1746. Of the Assembly's request, Franklin wrote: "They were respectable men of good understanding, but such was the 'State of Literature in Jersey' at the time that not one of them was capable of writing a proper answer." Franklin is supposed to have written such an excellent response that the Assembly hired him to print many of its official papers.[3]

When Collins prepared to open his shop in Burlington, he had to acquire the basic equipment common to every eighteenth-century "printing house," as such shops were known in the trade. The absolute necessities included at least one press and several sizes of type, two or three pairs of chases, galleys of folio and quarto dimensions, and numerous accessories in addition to ink and paper. Whatever could not be obtained from fellow printers or craftsmen in this country must be ordered from suppliers abroad who specialized in the making of printing equipment and supplies. Some items, such as the small pieces of "furniture" used to hold the type firmly in chases, could be manufactured locally, for example by artisans in Burlington.

A new press, made in England or Holland, the primary sources of printing equipment, would have cost Collins a tidy sum, and, therefore, he probably considered ordering his press from Christopher Sower, the Elder, of Germantown or Isaac Doolittle of New Haven, both of whom built presses before 1770. In 1769, the year Collins worked for William Goddard in Philadelphia, Goddard ordered a new mahogany press from Doolittle, supposedly the first made to order by an American craftsman for an American printer. Some printers, like Sower, constructed presses solely for their own use, but there is little reason to believe that Collins did this. It is most probable that he acquired a second- or third-hand press from an American printer able to invest in a new one.

Printing houses in eighteenth-century America were identified by the number of presses—one, two, or three—required for the work of the printer. In the beginning Collins's was of the "one press" variety, aptly described by Franklin in 1753 when he opened a small printing office in New Haven to be operated eventually by James Parker. From William Caslon, the famous English type-designer and typefounder, Franklin ordered the following type: long primer, with figures and signs sufficient for printing an almanac; pica; English; great primer; double pica; two-line English; and two-line great primer. He ordered 300 pounds each of long primer, pica, and English, sizes most frequently used. Franklin said he needed 100 pounds of great primer, 60 of double pica, 50 of two-line English, and 40 of two-line great primer. Finally, he specified that all the type should be in both Roman and italic, to be shipped with a variety of typographical ornaments for decorative purposes.[4] The type sizes Franklin purchased to equip the new shop ranged from 10 to 36 points, according to our modern system of type measurements.

The scant records fail to reveal where Collins acquired type for his shop. Among the early American type foundries, those operated by Abel Buell in Connecticut, David Mitchelson in Boston, and Christopher Sower, the Younger, in Germantown are considered the forerunners. Buell cast type in 1768 and 1769, the first American effort, but it was several years before he supplied type on a regular basis to printers. (He is known to have counterfeited money before he discovered a more honest and equally clever way of making a living.) Mitchelson's foundry was also experimental in about 1770. Sower's primary interest was in German letter for another edition of the Bible in German, and it was cast from imported matrices by two journeymen, Justus Fox and Jacob Bay, beginning about 1770. Fox and Bay, the first known typefounders in the Philadelphia area, very soon began cutting and casting Roman letter, but fonts of their manufacture could hardly have been available when Collins opened his shop in Burlington. It was not uncommon, however, for printers to borrow type from other printers, and Collins may have chosen this way of starting his business.

He must at least have tried to avoid the great expense of importing printing equipment and supplies from abroad. In 1760, for instance, Franklin paid Caslon the exorbitant price of £43 2s. 6d. for a font of new brevier for newspaper use, and other type sizes were required by even the smallest shop. Transportation fees alone accounted for a substantial part of the total cost of buying equipment abroad, and so it was with great anticipation that early American printers awaited the native development of the trades upon which they depended so much.

Considering the fact that the British pound sterling was worth from fifty to seventy percent more in purchasing power than the currencies of the various colonies in the mid-1800's, it is almost impossible to estimate the cost of printing equipment in contemporary terms. It is generally accepted, however, that the average value of a new one-press shop around the middle of the century was £85 sterling, roughly the equivalent of £125 in colonial currency. Caslon's charge to Franklin was exorbitant; the cost of this one font of type was more than half the value of an entire one-press shop. But no matter how one looks at the monetary exchange problem, which became even more complicated in the second half of the century, the master printer's expenses were high.

Between 1770 and 1775, American printers could begin to realize more economy in their business as the result of the increasing number of native suppliers. This was particularly true in regard to paper, which more and more was being manufactured in the colonies. Quality of the products, however, was another matter, a problem that only time and experience would solve.[5]

Collins, in an advertisement dated August 10, 1770, in the *Pennsylvania Gazette,* reported that he had "met with Encouragement, from a number of the most *respectable* Gentlemen in New-Jersey" and had moved his printing office from Philadelphia to Burlington. He said he had stocked a small assortment of books and stationery at his office, a one-room building at 206 High Street, the one formerly used by Franklin. Soon, as promised in the same notice, the newly arrived printer introduced New Jerseyans to the *Burlington Almanack,* the first of its kind to be published in the colony though not the first to circulate there.

The almanac, though it sold for only a few pennies, was a dependable money-maker, especially for printers like Collins who operated small, one-press establishments. If some households had no books, except perhaps the Bible and some basic religious tracts, all were obliged to own an almanac. Even among the illiterates and the poor it was popular. A Boston printer once boasted that his almanac had 60,000 subscribers and, we may assume, uncounted additional readers. By way of comparison, William Goddard's *Pennsylvania Chronicle* had the second largest newspaper circulation in the colonies in 1770 with 2,500 subscribers. "A person without an almanac," one bit of wisdom says, "is somewhat like a ship without a compass; he never knows what to do, nor when to do it." [6] Every colonial printer who was also a wise business-man produced at least one, sometimes as many as three or four, a year. It was the custom of almanac printers to attribute their authorship to English astrologers or philomaths such as Richard Saunders (Poor Richard), William Andrews (Poor Will), and William Winstanley (Poor Robin), or to use pseudonyms such as Abraham Weatherwise and Theophilus Grew. Some, on the other hand, like Daniel, Titan, and Felix Leeds and John Jerman, wrote under their own names. Collins's almanac-makers over the years were Timothy Trueman, William Waring, and Abraham Shoemaker.

As the "one universal book," the almanac was introduced to America from England in the mid-seventeenth century. Basically, it had three parts, or devices: the "kalendar," an ecclesiastical tabulation of days, weeks, and months with notations of Saints' days, feasts, and church festivals; the "almanack," an astronomical, and often astrological, computation of the passage of time; and the "prognostication," a mixture of popular fantasy, superstition, and politics. Much of this had been altered by 1770, but the mass appeal of the almanac was still strong.[7]

The *Burlington Almanack* for 1771 went on sale at the

Collins printing office on September 24, 1770, two months before Collins's former partner, Joseph Crukshank, offered *Poor Will's Almanack* from Philadelphia for the first time. Collins had learned to set type for these annual publications in James Adams's shop in Wilmington. The *Wilmington Almanack,* in fact, circulated in New Jersey, as did others from New York and Philadelphia. Still the most popular was *Poor Richard's* "improved" and published in 1770 by the firm of Hall and Sellers. Hugh Gaine's *Hutchins's* almanac, principally a New York publication, had many items of interest to New Jersey residents.

Similar in appearance and content to the others, the *Burlington Almanack* provided information about the motions of the sun and moon, "the true Places and Aspects of the Planets," the rising and setting of the sun and moon, weather forecasts, festivals and other "remarkable Days," and, of course, "High Water at Philadelphia." It also offered hints on health, together with a "Variety of useful and entertaining Matter." As was customary, the dates of Quaker meetings were listed, and the reader could turn to Timothy Trueman for the names of members of the New Jersey Council and Assembly and the dates and places of various judicial sessions around the province. In short, it was a pocketful of information on the seasons, agriculture, education of youth, marriage, solitude, integrity, and "the pleasures and advantages of society with the fair sex."

Printers used their almanacs to advertise other books and products on sale at their printing offices. Collins, for instance, advertised a supply of Bibles, spelling books, primers, writing paper, quills, ink powder, and sealing wax. He also appealed, as did other printers, for rags for making paper. In exchange he promised "Goods or Cash." When the shortage of rags became acute during the war, Collins advised New Jersey women: "It is customary in Great-Britain for Women who sew to have a small bag hanging to the Backs of their Chairs, into which they put their Cuttings even to the smallest Shred."

As the almanac went to press Collins was no doubt preoccupied by his expectation of succeeding James Parker as New Jersey's official government printer. Parker had died on July 2, 1770, and in September Collins set out to win the legislative commission to fill the vacant post. A similar petition was presented to the Assembly by Parker's son, Samuel, who on September 28, two days after the opening of the 21st Assembly's third session, at Perth Amboy, announced that he planned to continue his father's business in Woodbridge, near Perth Amboy, and desired, therefore, to be named public printer. Collins's petition was read before the Assembly the next day. Both petitions were tabled for a second reading, but on October 1, as recommendations from inhabitants of Middlesex and Essex counties were submitted to the legislators, support for Parker seemed to mount.[8]

Support for Collins held, and on October 2, as expected, he managed to acquire ten of the eighteen votes cast by the Assemblymen in what is recorded as New Jersey's first contest for government printing. Behind him, as anticipated, were the Smiths and, presumably, general enthusiasm in West Jersey. What actually took place in terms of political bargaining is not known. Religion, always a potent though intangible force in controversial issues, particularly in colonial America, may have influenced the balloting, but it is likely that the traditional separation of the province into East and West weighed heaviest, for the voting followed special interest lines. Of the Assemblymen who voted, eleven represented counties usually considered part of West Jersey. Representatives from Perth Amboy and Cape May county did not vote, but had they done so, it is reasonable to assume that Parker and Collins would each have received another vote. Because of recent deaths, Essex, Salem, and Cumberland counties, the last two of which were in West Jersey, were represented by two, instead of three, Assemblymen. Stephen Crane of Essex voted for Parker, and Ebenezer Miller, who alone represented the two western counties, voted for Collins. Their voting typified the contest.

The other votes for Parker came from Assemblymen from Middlesex, Monmouth, and Bergen counties in East Jersey. Interestingly, Samuel Tucker, a Trenton merchant who represented Hunterdon, Morris, and Sussex counties, broke with his colleague, John Hart, to vote for Parker. Hart, who was later one of the signers of the Declaration of Independence, voted for Collins. This was the only case of split voting. Collins had solid support from Assemblymen in Gloucester and Burlington counties, as well as from the city of Burlington. As the two seats of government, Perth Amboy and Burlington were the only cities permitted representation in the Assembly. What may have been the deciding votes came from Somerset County, the home of both farmers and merchants whose politics were divided, for Assemblymen Hendrick Fisher and John Berrien cast their votes for Collins.

Collins's commission proclaimed him "assigned, constituted and appointed . . . Printer for our Province . . .

Together with all Salaries, Fees, Perquisites, Profits, Privileges and Advantages to the said Office belonging or in any way appertaining, for and during our will and pleasure." [9] In essence, he was printer to King George III. The part about "our will and pleasure," which placed the printer at the mercy of the government and, possibly, its self-appointed censors, would later be tested, and weakened, as the storm of unrest throughout America threatened the status of the monarch's several colonial printers.

At the same time that it commissioned Collins, the Assembly ordered its new printer to publish 604 sets of its Votes and Proceedings and 569 copies of the legislative laws. Collins was also directed to distribute copies of each imprint to the governor, the treasurers of East and West Jersey, and to each Assemblyman, county clerk, town mayor, corporation executive, Council member, and judge. The committee assigned the responsibility of liaison with the government printer consisted of Fisher, Crane, Abraham Hewlings from the city of Burlington, and Henry Paxson from Burlington County. Hewlings, it appears, became Collins's principal contact with his employers.

Having won his commission, one of the most coveted prizes in the printing trade, Collins returned to work. The bulk of his working hours during 1770, as in later years, was spent on printing for the colonial government. Had he depended on the sale of his almanac, lucrative as this aspect of the trade was, he would have gone out of business in a short time. Estimates are that government work for commissioned printers brought from £200 to £300 sterling a year, a considerable sum for the time. Benjamin Franklin's "first Promotion" was his selection as clerk of the Pennsylvania General Assembly in 1736, because he valued the opportunity of securing public printing contracts for his press. "Besides the Pay for immediate Service as Clerk," Franklin wrote in his autobiography, "the Place gave me a better Opportunity of keeping up an Interest among the Members, which secur'd to me the Business of Printing the Votes, Laws, Paper Money, and other occasional Jobbs for the Public, that on the whole were very profitable." [10] Public printing, in short, meant security for printers in an otherwise insecure business.

In addition to the almanac, Collins printed during the remaining few months of his first year in Burlington an English translation of Jean-François Marmontel's *History of Belisarius, the Heroik and Humane Roman General*. From booksellers' advertisements, one may conclude that Marmontel ranked high among the numerous French authors popular in eighteenth-century America. *Belisarius* and Fénelon's *Adventures of Telemachus*, which detail the qualities of good rulers and soldiers, are believed to have had considerable influence on early political thought in America.[11]

With the publication of his first book in Burlington, Collins had started on the road to becoming more than a mere printer. However, the distinction between *bookseller* and *publisher*, except in cases of printers who published newspapers, was not always as clear in the eighteenth century as it is today. Often these technical terms, meaningful within the trade, were used interchangeably. "Stated in its simplest terms, the difference between bookseller and publisher is not the difference between one man and another but the difference between the roles that one

35

man is playing in getting books into the hands of the purchaser. If the proprietor of a bookshop owns the copyright of a book, seeks out a printer for it, and then manages the sale to the public, his role is that of *bookseller*. If, on the other hand, the author (or printer) owns the copyright and secures the services of the proprietor of a bookshop in selling a book, then that proprietor is in the role of *publisher*." [12]

Bookshop proprietors who were not attached to a printing house often played the role of booksellers exclusively. In general, however, they acted at times as booksellers, at others as publishers. Collins was primarily a printer, but, like most colonial printers, he sometimes served as a publisher of books. On other occasions, which are sometimes difficult to determine from the title pages of books he printed, he served technically as a bookseller. In any event, the importance of diversification, in Collins's time as now, is explained somewhat in a letter written in 1771 by the successful London printer William Strahan to his friend David Hall in Philadelphia. "I quickly saw," he explained, "that if I confined myself to mere *printing for Booksellers* I might be able to live, but very little more than live, I therefore soon determined to launch out into other Branches in Connection with my own, in which I have happily succeeded, to the Astonishment of the rest of the Trade here, who never dreamt of going out of the old beaten Track. Thus I have made the Name of *Printer* more respectable than ever it was before, and taught them to emancipate themselves from the Slavery in which the Booksellers held them." [13]

Another staple of the colonial press was the printed sermon. Collins issued several over the years, the first written by Thomas Bradbury Chandler, minister of St. John's church in Elizabethtown. Printed by Collins on contract for the Anglican denomination, Chandler's sermon had been delivered on the anniversary of the Corporation for the Relief of the Widows and Children of Clergymen in the Communion of the Church of England in America. Usually in the Middle Colonies the practice was to publish mainly those sermons given at special celebrations. New England printers, by contrast, issued quantities of sermons, in response to popular demand.

Chandler's sermon was printed in a seventy-six-page pamphlet bound with an abstract to the proceedings of the corporation's annual meeting held October 2, 1771, in Perth Amboy. Collins, in this case, worked for the corporation, which in turn sold copies of the sermon for the benefit of the relief fund. What the printer charged for the printing of such pamphlets is nearly impossible to ascertain, but his fees were probably in the range of twenty to twenty-five shillings per sheet, or page, the trade's average rate during most of the eighteenth century. Since labor costs were a major expense for the printer, the charges for private printing largely depended upon the nature of the material to be printed. Tabular matter, for instance, required more time to set in type than an essay or a sermon.

By working under contract on the Chandler sermon, Collins, who may or may not have been enthusiastic himself about its contents or its general acceptance by his book customers, risked no financial embarrassment. Though these publications appealed mainly to the clergy and perhaps to their own parishioners, admonitory discourses were frequently purchased in large quantities by people of other denominations.[14]

One of the most curious little books ever to come from a colonial press was Robert Dodsley's *Oeconomy of Human Life,* an edition of which Collins issued in 1771, some twenty years after it had been introduced to American readers by Daniel Fowle of Boston. It contained various precepts, maxims, and aphorisms discussed under the subjects of Modesty, Prudence, Emulation, Love, Women, Husband, Father, and Temperance. The volume went through no less than forty separate editions in this country before 1800, evidence of its popularity as a behavior guide.

Dodsley, a famous London bookseller and writer, is said to have collaborated with Lord Chesterfield in the authorship. During the twelve months following its first London printing *Oeconomy of Human Life,* the title of which would itself attract some interest, was reissued by Franklin and Hall in Philadelphia and by James Parker in New York, as well as by Fowle. Therefore, Collins, it is clear, simply included among his early New Jersey offerings a book that would guarantee substantial sales and profit.[15]

His only other book imprint for 1771 was Thomas Moody's *Compendium of Surveying,* a small ready reckoner, a "pocket companion," with several charts and mathematical tables for the plotting of land either by the professional or by the amateur surveyor. Here again Collins printed the book expressly for the author. Advertisements noted that copies could be purchased directly from Moody as well as from the Burlington print shop. By the end of his first full year in Burlington, Collins had issued a total of fourteen imprints, most, of course, ordered by the New Jersey legislature.

The printer was not occupied in the shop all the time. In the front of the building he maintained a notions department, featuring merchandise not normally found in similar business establishments. Because of its newsy and curious atmosphere, Collins's place was a center of community activity. On his shelves, besides the stationery and printed matter, townspeople, buyers or just browsers, could find Godfrey's cordial, Say's balsam, Bateman's pectoral drops, Daffy's elixir, and Hooper's female pills. Chocolate, lemons, pens, and tea were also stocked. Always, of course, the town's more learned citizens could purchase an assortment of books taken on consignment by the printer from publishers in other colonies, England, and France.

Isaac Collins's courtship of Rachel Budd, begun in Philadelphia, led to their marriage on May 8, 1771. According to the custom still practiced among Quakers, they "declared intentions" at monthly meetings in March and April, after which permission to marry was officially granted.[16] Their marriage certificate bore the signatures of numerous friends and relatives, many of whom were prominent Quakers, who witnessed the ceremony at the Bank Meeting House in Philadelphia. Among these were John Pemberton, Thomas Scattergood, Owen Jones, Moses Bartram, Stacy and Joseph Budd, Dr. James Hutchinson, Dr. Benjamin Say, and his son Thomas, the naturalist and writer. An old friend and mentor, William Goddard, published a simple report in his *Chronicle:* "Married . . . Mr. Isaac Collins of Burlington, Printer, to Miss Rachel Budd, of this City." [17]

Both turned from traditional Quaker costume for the wedding. Rachel wore a light blue brocade; her matching shoes had very high heels, not larger than a gold dollar, and sharply pointed toes. Her robe-style outfit was long in the back with a large hoop, and her short blue bodice had a white satin stomacher embroidered in colors, with a blue cord laced from side to side. She wore a black hood lined with white silk, and a large cape extending over her shoulders. Isaac wore a coat of peach-blossom cloth with patch pockets on the skirts, lined with elaborately quilted white silk. He also wore silver knee buckles, white silk stockings, pumps, and a three-cornered beaver hat. It is said that the style of dress worn by Rachel was the same as that of Hannah Logan, daughter of the distinguished Philadelphian, James Logan, at her marriage to John Smith.[18]

Rachel Budd was a member of a ranking Philadelphia Quaker family. On the paternal side she was descended from the Rev. Thomas Budd, once an Anglican minister in England, who had renounced his faith and become an active member of the Society of Friends. A great-uncle, John Budd, was an early Quaker in Burlington; he helped build the town's first meeting house in 1683. Rachel's father, Thomas, was a wealthy Philadelphia merchant. On the maternal side, Rachel's mother, Rebecca, also came from a family of eminent Quakers. She was the great-granddaughter of Mahlon Stacy, an early settler of Trenton, New Jersey. Isaac's sister, Elizabeth, was the only Collins at the wedding.

The newlyweds started housekeeping in an old hipped-roof house at the southeast corner of High and Union Streets in Burlington, a town at that time still saddened by the death of John Smith in March. In New Jersey alone, not taking into account his earlier mercantile reputation in Pennsylvania, Smith had contributed time and money to public services, philanthropies, and literary pursuits. He had been an important member of the Burlington Monthly Meeting, where Isaac and Rachel were "received" on June 28.[19]

In his business Collins was of increasing value to the Society of Friends, at least in terms of the publication of pamphlets, epistles, and books by Quaker authors. This tie between a merchant and his religious denomination, which for Collins seems to have tightened as the years went by, was not unique in early America. The religious element had perhaps entered into Collins's decision to move from Williamsburg to Philadelphia, but then Philadelphia was a printing capital as well as a Quaker stronghold, and close to the countryside in which he had grown up.

Three antislavery writers who had stimulated action within the Society of Friends to free Negroes were John Woolman, Anthony Benezet, and Granville Sharp, whose manuscripts Collins published in 1772 and 1773. Woolman, who lived near Burlington in Mount Holly, New Jersey, often visited the former town. In his writings he had argued that slaveholding dulled both sympathy and the moral sense and "produced a general decline of godly conduct wherever it prevailed." [20] Collins issued works by Benezet and Sharp in 1773.

Out of the reform movement within the Society against slaveholding grew Benezet's *Brief Consideration on Slavery, and the Expediency of Its Abolition,* which bears Collins's imprint. The year before, Joseph Crukshank had issued Benezet's *A Mite Cast into the Treasure; or, Observations on Slave-Keeping,* one of several works by the author published by Collins's former business associate. Collins became acquainted with Benezet in Philadelphia. A native of France, born into a Huguenot family which escaped to London and then migrated to Philadelphia in 1731, Benezet had published three important books on the slave trade before he hired Collins to print the fourth.

An equally important Quaker admonition printed by Collins in 1773 was Sharp's *An Essay on Slavery, Proving from Scripture Its Inconsistency with Humanity and Religion,* a book as timely today as it must have been in the eighteenth century. Sharp wrote the essay to confute, as he put it, a piece by a British clergyman, Rev. Thomas Thompson, entitled, "The African trade for Negro Slaves shewn to be consistent with principles of humanity, and with the laws of revealed religion." Sharp maintained, as did Woolman and Benezet, that slavery is contrary both to the laws of reason and to the principles of "revealed religion."

By issuing these publications Collins probably did as much as, or more than, most Quaker printers in the colonies toward the dissemination of information about the "iniquitous practice of buying, selling or keeping Slaves." [21] Not all colonial printers are known to have accepted manuscripts from Quaker reformers. It would seem that Collins was in step with the general moral revival among Quakers that enabled them eventually to forbid slaveholding on pain of disownment.[22] He early freed his own Negro slave.

The religious work from Collins's press was not confined to the writings of Quakers. Richard Baxter's Puritan masterpiece, *The Saint's Everlasting Rest*—considered comparable in value to anything prepared by John Cotton—and William Mason's *Methodism Displayed* are notable among the non-Quaker books Collins printed. A wise businessman, Collins knew that any book or collection of sermons from Baxter's pen enjoyed great popularity in the colonies and should find some new buyers in Burlington.

Since late in 1771, with the help of Crukshank, Collins had been working toward a reprinting of Willem Sewel's monumental *History of the Rise, Increase and Progress of the Christian People Called Quakers,* a job which took more than two years to complete. Their assignment had been initiated by the Philadelphia Meeting for Sufferings at a time when there seems to have been increasing general interest among Quakers in the history of their sect.[23] In December 1771 Collins and Crukshank notified the Society's standing business committee of their willingness to reissue an edition of Sewel. Next, they proposed a subscription plan for assuring the printing and the sale of a thousand copies. The Philadelphia Yearly Meeting, whose clerk was John Pemberton, voted to give the assignment to Collins (whether with or without the further help of Crukshank is not clear), and work was under way by the following summer.

"I am glad a Committee is appointed to assist in getting the Paper," Collins wrote Pemberton, "which will save the Mind of Thy respectful Friend." Appointed liaison between the printer and the special Quaker committee was Dr. Benjamin Say, whom Collins affectionately called "Father Say." In the same letter to Pemberton,

Collins called attention to his profound worry over the availability of paper and said that he would check periodically with the committee for advice.[24]

By January 1773 he was well enough along with the composition of type for Sewel's masterpiece to make a full report to Pemberton. First, he said the subscription price "must be 20s." Second, he had consulted with a Wilmington bookbinder, John Hall, "who says he could readily bind 1000 Pages together." When finished, the book came to less than 850 pages. Third, Collins had given proof sheets (page proofs), "in compliance to the Request of the Meeting," to Samuel Smith, the historian, and George Dillwyn, a personal friend and Quaker spokesman. Finally, the printer reported that he had to pay Jacob Hagy nine shillings a ream for paper. But, "as it is not so good as he gave me Reason to expect," Collins said he wanted no more of Hagy's paper.[25]

For bindery work Collins usually looked to craftsmen in Philadelphia and Wilmington. From the start the prominent Philadelphia binder Robert Aitken appears to have handled a large portion of Collins's work. For instance, Aitken did the major part of the Sewel job while Hall bound several volumes. During one period, eleven months in 1774 and 1775, Aitken bound in either sheep or calf and lettered and filleted more than 1,400 Sewel books for Collins. The number, greater than Collins had expected to print, is nevertheless evidence of the book's quality and lasting popularity.[26]

By the 1770's the bookbinding business in America had taken on new importance; it had become a highly skilled craft and it was now generally a separate enterprise from bookselling and printing in the large cities. The basic materials and techniques, however, were relatively unchanged since the seventeenth century. Plain white or colored paper was used to cover the normal issue of the printing shop, e.g., almanacs, session laws and assembly proceedings, pamphlets, and sermons. Vellum or parchment made cheap and durable covers, but calf was the leather most favored for the more substantial works. Specially processed sheep (sprinkled or marbled) and imported morocco, the Turkish goatskin which was increasingly being replaced by less expensive domestic imitations, were used when the customer or the binder wanted a book to appear elegant. The endpapers were often flowered or marbled.

Printers like Collins, who did not bind their own imprints, commonly ordered books bound "plain" or "gilt," which meant that the decorations on the boards and spine were tooled either "blind" or in gold leaf. Aitken, who was also one of Collins's sources of ink powders, paper, parchment, and used type, bound most of the Sewel books in sheep, blind-tooled and lettered, at a cost of 7s. 9d. per volume. When Collins ordered calf, which he did but few times, he was charged an additional 4s. 6d. per volume.[27]

Besides Aitken and Hall, the two who seem to have bound most of the Sewel books, Collins's binders over the years were James Wilson and the firm of Craig and Lea, both of Wilmington, Conrad Seyfert and Muir and Hyde of Philadelphia, and James Leishman (or Lishman). Leishman had worked for Aitken and in 1775 or 1776 moved to Burlington as a bookbinder and bookseller. While he was with Aitken he no doubt was responsible for much of the work done for Collins and thus got to know the Burlington printer. The first evidence in

Aitken's waste-book that he had left his master and moved to New Jersey is the Burlington entry for May 13, 1775, charging Leishman eighteen shillings for one morocco skin. Later Leishman followed Collins to Trenton.

Sewel's *History* had first been printed in 1717 in Dutch, the author's native tongue. An English version, printed in 1722, sold widely in Great Britain and America. Before the historian's death in 1725 he had managed to write three corrected editions; it was the last of these from which Collins printed. The appearance of the volume under Collins's imprint on the eve of the Revolution was timed to coincide with the Quaker reform movement, which looked ahead to future generations firmly rooted in tradition. "To those convinced that their ancestors had set a model of conduct, laxity in their own day constituted a grave declension." [28] The Quaker ways of plainness and pacifism were about to be put to a severe test in the young country.

With the Sewel imprint about completed in October 1773, Collins wrote again to Pemberton. He reported that he had received a total of 492 reams of paper from Frederick Bicking and 512 from Hagy. Collins said Bicking had been paid, indicating that he had replaced Hagy (whose account was settled) as supplier sometime during the printing process. Next to the cost of labor, expenditures for paper made up the major expense of the colonial printer. Collins's displeasure over having to pay Hagy and the others nine shillings a ream is perhaps understandable, since the price was only ten to twelve shillings for the period 1730–1747 covered by Franklin's *Account Books*. By the time Collins set up business in

Burlington more than thirty years later, there were about fifteen paper mills in the Philadelphia area alone, so that competition might logically have reduced the price. Furthermore, as Wroth notes, the average cost of ordinary printing paper manufactured in America "seems to have lessened as the years advanced." [29] But a drop of one to three shillings over thirty years could hardly be called a lessening. As Collins had complained to Pemberton, nine shillings "is more than the Worth of it—as paper is commonly sold." [30]

The implications of the printer's distress go much deeper. Despite the growth in the number of paper mills, the product was usually in short supply because of the lack of rags. More will be said on this problem as it relates to Collins's newspaper, but here it may be noted that during 1773, the same year that Collins encountered difficulty in acquiring paper for Sewel's book, a group of Philadelphia printers, among them Collins's former partner, Joseph Crukshank, launched an unusual appeal to the public. Supported by the influential American Philosophical Society, the printers announced in the *Pennsylvania Gazette* that they had provided prize money as premiums to encourage the public to save and collect linen rags for the manufacturing of white paper. "Everywhere the making of paper . . . brought about a valuable spirit of cooperation among all elements of the community." [31] Despite the location of a paper mill in Perth Amboy by 1772, Collins was virtually not able to buy paper in New Jersey until 1776 and 1777, when mills opened in Burlington, Trenton, and Spotswood, near New Brunswick. Until he could turn to these mills, Collins depended upon suppliers from the other side of the Delaware.

As for his labor force, publishing the Sewel book, a considerable job even by today's standards, would in itself have required additional workers. During 1773 Collins advertised for, and presumably hired, at least one pressman, an apprentice, and a journeyman printer, "recommended for sobriety and steadiness to business." [32] Wages being generally fixed during the second half of the eighteenth century, Collins paid his printer sixpence for setting a thousand letters of type. Journeyman printers were paid according to the kind of job and its size in terms of paper and type used. For instance, setting a folio-size job would normally bring about twice the earnings of one quarto-size. Pressmen were paid twelve pence a "token," 240 sheets printed on one side, "which is too much, if Pressmen had constant Work, as Compositors; but in America Numbers being generally small, they must often stand still, and often make ready." [33]

One of Collins's early employees was Benjamin Franklin's nephew, Benjamin Mecom. This wandering printer, generally unsuccessful in business for himself, yet amicable by nature, was born in Boston and apprenticed to James Parker in New Haven at the age of thirteen. Even then he showed signs of eccentricity, and seven years later he was off to Antigua to establish a printing office for his uncle. Mecom married a New Jersey girl and, according to Isaiah Thomas, returned to the province for his declining days. Just before moving to Burlington, he had failed with his own shop in Philadelphia. Thomas remembered Mecom as a man of ingenuity and integrity, a correct and skillful printer.

But, Thomas admits, Mecom was "deficient in the art of managing business to profit." Thomas knew Mecom from both their days in Boston, and gives us this description: "He was handsomely dressed, wore a powdered bob wig, ruffles and gloves; gentlemanlike appendages which the printers of that day did not assume, and thus apparelled, would often assist for an hour, at the press. He indeed put on an apron to save his clothes from blacking, and guarded his ruffles; but he wore his coat, his wig, his hat and his gloves, whilst working at press; and at case, laid aside his apron." [34]

Collins no doubt met Mecom when they were both working for William Goddard. His years of experience would have been valuable to the growing Burlington printing shop and its young master. For instance, Mecom once published a magazine and was the first American printer to attempt stereotype printing, the process for casting curved plates in lead for rotary printing. He was a gentleman in appearance and manners, Thomas wrote, and "had been well educated in his business, and if *queer,* was honest and sensible." [35]

In the capacity of master printer Collins was thrown into the legislature's problem of colonial finances in the days when New Jersey was devoid of "hard money"— gold or silver—and the balance of trade was highly in favor of England. In March 1774, after the Assembly had passed a law to establish a loan office and issue paper money, Collins and a South Carolina printer, Thomas Powell, underwent questioning by the lawmakers relative to the mode of printing the bills of credit. Collins testified that he had access to a press that could print four bills on one piece of paper, saving time and paper "not easily to be had." He said he knew of "Types enough to print all the Bills of this and the neighboring Colonies," but he believed there was a limited number of denominational ornaments or plates. He admitted he did not understand printing with a copper plate, a method in which he had little faith anyway, "too many being ill-done." [36]

Once the emission was authorized, the act was sent to England for the King's approval, which finally came late the following year. During the interim a convention of delegates from several counties had assembled at New Brunswick to place the province in readiness for combat should the need arise. So-called Committees of Correspondence, sparked by the Boston Port Act of May 10, 1774, sprang up in all the colonies in an effort to unify the actions of their assemblies. Essex County was the first to organize in New Jersey, on June 11, led by William Livingston, William Peartree Smith, Elias Boudinot, Stephen Crane, and John DeHart.

The final meeting of the old Assembly was in November 1775, and the newly formed Provincial Congress voted during the following February to issue £50,000 in bills of credit. Collins, as public printer, was directed to print the various denominations as soon as possible. They bore the admonition "To counterfeit is death." [37] At this time, during the awkward change in governments, there were two distinct legislative powers in New Jersey, both claiming and exercising power, with several members of one being also members of the other. As legal printer to the King, Collins continued to abide by the conditions of his commission. As printer to the elected Assembly also, he was obligated to serve the public. Therefore, in name only was he printer to King George. Collins and his workmen were close witnesses to the Revolution as it evolved in print. We can imagine, for example, the printing shop in the closing months of 1775 and the early months of 1776: type being composed for the "ordinances" of the Provincial Congress simultaneously with impressions being made of the "laws" of the old Assembly.[38]

During the period Collins was printing the new currency, his shop produced only two significant volumes: George Fisher's *The American Instructor,* a school book of "spelling, reading, writing, and arithmetick, in an easier way than any yet published," issued in 1775, and a compilation of New Jersey laws, finished in 1776. Samuel Allinson, a Burlington Quaker who served as surrogate for West Jersey, had been appointed by the legislature in 1773 to collect and publish a new edition of the laws. Collins did the printing in a folio edition of more than five hundred pages.

Collins's account with New Jersey from May 20 to November 18, 1776, reflects some of the political and military developments within the province as it struggled to become a state. From his printing press in May came 100 copies of various resolutions of the Committee of Safety, an appointed group with certain legal powers to act when Congress was not in session. The resolutions called mainly for the organization of a militia. In June, with the British invasion imminent, Collins printed more than 800 copies of the ordinances for raising 3,300 men for the militia, including an order for dispatching men to help fortify New York. The printer also issued 150 copies of ordinances directing the election of a new Provincial Congress, which ultimately convened at Burlington on June 10. On July 6 Collins finished printing 1,000 copies of New Jersey's first state constitution, which the Provincial Congress had adopted four days before. In the same month the Congress took action against what it called "Non-Associators" and announced through Collins's press that they were to be disarmed. Throughout most of the following year Collins's press was kept busy with ordinances, proclamations, and circular letters designed to encourage enlistments in the militia and to discourage traitors and "disaffected persons." [39]

More than five years had elapsed since Collins's election to the post of government printer, about the same length of time he had been master of the Burlington printing house. For the most part, it was possible for a Quaker businessman to divide his loyalties, as one historian puts it, between the counting house and the meeting house.[40] But for a Quaker who also served part of the time as an official of a provincial government, loyalties were not so easily defined. Most Friends maintained an attitude of aloofness from the ways of the new government, while others leaned toward Toryism, not necessarily because of particular faith in the Crown, but rather because they believed more strongly in a "peaceable testimony." As a body, they reaffirmed this principle in January 1775. Circumstances of the time, however, prevailed upon Collins to favor the affairs of state over the affairs of religion.

Evidence of his political sympathies is found in a brief letter he wrote on December 27, 1775, recommending a fellow printer, Shepard Kollock, for a commission in the Continental Army. Collins added in the postscript: "This is the first time perhaps that ever a person of my Profession recommended a Man for such an office. But such is the Idea I have of *Public Justice & self Defense.*" From a long acquaintance with his colleague, he said he believed Kollock "to be a young fellow of good principles and resolution, and he appears to be hearty in the American cause." [41]

A more significant test of Collins's politics came several months later, in June 1776, when, in the midst of New Jersey's government changeover, he refused to publish a long address Governor William Franklin had written to the Council and Assembly. The New Jersey Provincial Congress, in finding Franklin in contempt of the Continental Congress by being in violation of its resolution to suppress "every kind of government under the Crown," had ordered his arrest.[42] He was denied the opportunity to defend himself in person before the legislators, and instead wrote out the address in the form of a letter, which essentially attacked the patriots.

This was on June 17. Five days later, in a postscript added in Burlington after he had talked at length with Collins, the embattled governor wrote: "But though he [Collins] at first gave me expectations that he would do his duty (as all good Officers ought to do, or resign their commissions) he afterwards returned it, declaring that he was afraid of offending the Provincial Congress, and that he did not doubt but he should be killed if he should print it for me, with many more excuses of the like nature." Seemingly, Franklin enjoined a third party to intercede in his behalf, but "no argument could prevail," and Collins returned the letter.

Furthermore, Collins defied the governor's orders not to report the incident to the new legislature, for the lawmakers thereafter prohibited the publication of anything written by Franklin. "They can no more bear the light of truth, it seems, than owls can endure the light of the sun!"

Franklin said.[48] The letter eventually appeared in Hugh Gaine's *New-York Gazette and Weekly Mercury* for February 3, 1777.

Meanwhile, ensuing political and military events, many of which came to a climax in New Jersey, helped create the need for a newspaper in the newly independent state. Moreover, when a master printer equipped himself with an assortment of type and a press, he expected to turn out all kinds of printed matter—commercial forms and blanks, broadsides and pamphlets, schoolbooks and almanacs, laws, sermons, and books. To round out his enterprise he would expect to publish a newspaper, one of several ways the eighteenth-century printer could further assert himself in the community. During his years in Burlington Collins had turned out all but a newspaper.

❧ III ❧
NEWSPAPER
PUBLISHER

New Jersey was one of the last of the original colonies
to have a newspaper, although nearly forty were
being published when war broke out in the spring of 1775.
Fifteen were located in New England, as would be expected, thirteen in the Middle Colonies, and ten in the
south for an over-all ratio of one paper to every 60,000
to 65,000 people. Of the available newspapers, two were
in New Hampshire, seven in Massachusetts, four in Connecticut, two in Rhode Island, four in New York, seven
in Pennsylvania, two in Maryland, four in Virginia, two
in North Carolina, three in South Carolina, and one in
Georgia.[1]

The late establishment of a newspaper in New Jersey
is largely attributable to the fact that most New York and
Pennsylvania papers published news of interest to New

Jerseyans and circulated widely in the neighboring colony. But although it is true that New Jersey had little need for its own paper prior to the war, it is also true that Tory as well as Whig journals were read by New Jersey residents. James Rivington's *New-York Gazetteer,* to use the obvious example, had the largest circulation of any newspaper in the colonies for the critical years of 1774 and 1775, a large part of which was in New Jersey. Another predominantly Tory sheet, Hugh Gaine's *New-York Gazette and Weekly Mercury,* for a brief time was even printed in New Jersey.

Citizens were so aroused over the conflict with Great Britain that Rivington's paper was eventually boycotted in New Jersey as part of a greater intercolony campaign to force the printer out of business. Newark's Committee on Observation resolved in January 1775 "henceforth to take no more of his papers, pamphlets, or any other publick performance of his press." Residents of Morris County called Rivington an enemy of his country and vowed to discourage the circulation of his paper in their county. In Woodbridge, New Jersey, they said he was "a person inimical to the liberties of this country, and cordially recommended to all our constituents to drop his Paper and have no further dealings with him."

The anti-Rivington movement reached further into the center of the colony, where perhaps the most graphic demonstration occurred. Whigs in New Brunswick hanged the printer in effigy on April 13, 1775, and described him as a "noxious exotick plant, incapable either of cultivation or improvement in this soil of freedom." Amused by it all, Rivington published a drawing of the event in his *Gazetteer* for April 20. The expressions of indignation continued, and in November a party of New York Whigs raided his shop and destroyed his type and equipment. Rivington fled to England, but returned when the British held the city.[2]

Such feuds between the Tories and the Whigs, illustrated by Rivington's journalistic misfortunes, suggest the basic motivation for establishing a newspaper in New Jersey. If Rivingston's paper enjoyed as much influence as the reprisals against him would seem to indicate, then clearly the colony needed a journal more in harmony with Whig, or patriot, ideas. There were other reasons, however. As the patriot cause reached a crucial stage in the nearly disastrous winter of 1776–77, several papers serving New Jersey ceased publication. In Philadelphia, James Humphreys, because of his avowed Toryism, was forced to stop publishing his *Ledger* in 1776. Other publishers moved to distant points to escape British suppression. Furthermore, the manufacture of paper more than ever lagged behind printers' requirements, thus forcing subscription rates beyond an amount many people could pay. Particularly exasperating was the uncertainty of delivery by post-riders. For these reasons the need for a medium to disseminate news and information became more urgent by 1777, during the last month of which Collins began publishing the *New-Jersey Gazette*. Before this, however, there had been several attempts at publishing a periodical in the colony.

James Parker, the printer who had set up the first established press in New Jersey in 1751 in Woodbridge, was also affiliated with the first journalistic effort in the colony. Parker, appointed the colony's government printer in 1758, published the *New American Magazine* from his

Woodbridge shop between January of that year and March 1760. His editor and the main force behind the publication was Samuel Nevill, a London journalist who had moved to Perth Amboy in 1735. As for Parker's role, he was, according to Lyon N. Richardson, "primarily concerned with the venture only as a method of furnishing work for his Woodbridge printing establishment." [3] However, it is to Parker's credit that though he was not a writer himself he was one of those colonial printers who explored every conceivable aspect of his trade. Before he and Nevill launched the *New American Magazine*, Parker had acquired a reputation as a printer of newspapers and magazines in New York.

After having served his apprenticeship in the *New-York Gazette* office of the elder William Bradford, Parker established his own newspaper, the *New-York Weekly Post-Boy*, in 1743. Upon Bradford's retirement four years later, he acquired his former master's printing patronage and merged the two papers into the *New-York Gazette; or, the Weekly Post-Boy*. Then in November 1752 he added to his printing assignments the *Independent Reflector*, a militant journal edited by William Livingston, a young New York attorney who had been a literary contributor to the *Post-Boy* as early as 1745. But this arrangement soon ended abruptly, for Parker feared reprisals in his capacity of official printer to the New York legislature. However, he printed four numbers of another Livingston creation, the *Occasional Reverberator*, in the fall of 1753 and collaborated later with William Weyman in publishing two more short-lived magazines, *John Englishman* and the *Instructor*.

Parker's New York newspaper for August 29, 1757,

carried the announcement of the coming of the *New American Magazine,* to be issued from his Woodbridge, New Jersey, shop. Dated from Perth Amboy, the advertisement was probably written by Nevill. He said the magazine would be a monthly consisting of six half-sheets octavo and costing a shilling. It would be divided into two sections, the first being a "complete History of the *Northern Continent of America* . . . Compiled with that Impartiality and Regard to Truth which becomes a faithful Historian, and carefully extracted from Authors of the best Credit both ancient and modern." The second half would contain *"Amusements and Essays, serious, entertaining, philosophical, mechanical, historical, political* and *poetical,* with the most *material News* and *authentic Occurrences,* Foreign and Domestic, which shall happen during the Month." In addition, "whatsoever *New Pieces* any Gentlemen may be so kind to furnish us with, shall always have the Preference in our *Magazine,* out of a peculiar Emulation to satisfy the Publick that even this *New World* is not destitute of *Learning* and *Learned Men.*" [4] The magazine appeared, as promised, in January 1758 and according to specifications. But though it survived for two years and three months, the *New American Magazine* never had much success. Almost from the beginning original contributors and expected subscribers were few. As Richardson writes: "It never aspired to originality, being made up of reprints." [5]

It is likely that what sustained readers' interest for twenty-seven months was the first half of the magazine, which consisted of previously published works on history compiled by Nevill himself. The selections tended to favor a British point of view, but the editor's serious attitude toward history could have impressed a sufficient number of readers. Readers probably lost interest early in the material in the second half, where the proprietors had promised originality and never were able to fulfill their promise. Nevill admitted that some readers found much of the material "dull and burthensome." The prose contents may be divided into four broad categories: commentaries on the war and related matter of geography and the Indians; *belles-lettres,* pieces on science, and sentimental tales. Richardson's evaluation is accurate: "It is apparent that the *New American Magazine,* though edited without brilliance, was distinctive for its articles on history and the war, for the reprints selected by one familiar with editorial life in London, and for poetry definitely valuable to the student of a changing age." [6] Income failed to defray the cost of printing, and the magazine was discontinued with the issue of March 1760.

Clearer evidence that the colony wanted a revolutionary press of its own was Parker's plan to start one in Burlington. On April 25, 1765, he wrote to Benjamin Franklin, but mourned to his former associate that "the News of the Killing Stamp, has struck a deadly Blow to all my Hopes on that Head." [7] Five months later, however, William Goddard issued a protest against the Stamp Act from Parker's Woodbridge printing shop. It was the first and only number of a paper called the *Constitutional Courant,* published on September 21. A vigorous but not unusual piece of propaganda, the *Courant* stirred up a furor in New York, where most copies circulated, and in parts of New Jersey. But only by chance was the *Courant* a New Jersey product, despite the connection between Parker's plan and Goddard's effort sometime later. Goddard wrote to Isaiah Thomas that, though John Holt, a patriot printer in New York, helped him compile "several elegantly written and highly spirited essays, against the unjust tax," no printer in New York dared to publish them. "I volunteered my services, went to Woodbridge, and obtained leave to use the apparatus there at pleasure." [8] A few years later Thomas, publisher of the Whig *Massachusetts Spy,* was asked by a group of radicals to set up a press in New Jersey. It, like Parker's plan, never materialized.

Another attempt at journalism in New Jersey was the *Plain-Dealer,* which lasted for only eight issues between December 1775 and February 1776. The editors were four prominent New Jerseyans and avid patriots, Dr. Jonathan Elmer, Joseph Bloomfield, Dr. Lewis Howell and his brother Richard.

At least two of the men, Elmer and Richard Howell, had been connected with the colony's version of the Boston Tea Party, a "tea-burning" that took place in Greenwich, on the Cohansey River in Cumberland County, during the night of December 12, 1774. According to an old newspaper account, the following May an attempt was made to have a Cumberland County grand jury indict the leaders of the foray, but Elmer, then sheriff and a brother of one of the leaders, saw to it that a jury of Whigs was picked, with another brother as foreman. No indictments were made.[9] Bloomfield and Richard Howell later served New Jersey as governor, and Elmer became president of the New Jersey Medical Society and a United States senator.

The *Plain-Dealer* they edited was written in manuscript and posted in Matthew Potter's tavern in Bridgeton, a center of patriot activity. Each weekly issue contained one essay, "no number . . . to excel half a sheet in length"; topics varied, from politics, such as "the present unhappy dispute between Great Britain and America," to nonpolitics, such as the theory and practice of bundling. It was without current news and other traditional newspaper features. Indeed, the editors were native New Jerseyans and the paper lasted longer than the *Constitutional Courant,* but it did not circulate and could hardly be called a newspaper. Nonetheless, when the paper was reproduced more than a century later, it was identified as "The First Newspaper in New Jersey." [10]

For a few weeks in 1776 still a third newspaper carried a New Jersey colophon. Hugh Gaine, who had served as an apprentice under James Parker in New York and had then become one of that city's outstanding printers, published his *New-York Gazette and Weekly Mercury* from Newark during the fall of that year. He had moved part of his printing equipment across the Hudson just prior to the British occupation of New York. In Newark he issued seven weekly editions, beginning on September 21. However, he could not escape the familiar hindrances to printing—difficult political times, subscribers in arrears and scattered, paper nearly impossible to obtain, and, of course, the anticipated invasion of New Jersey itself. Displeased by his failure to find a new home for his newspaper, Gaine soon abandoned any plan he may have had for establishing a paper in New Jersey. After the edition of November 2 the printer returned to New York and became the city's leading Royalist publisher in the absence of the exiled James Rivington. Like Rivington, Gaine suffered abuse and jibes from the local patriot press. He was not a turncoat, but an opportunist who, unlike John Holt and other devoted patriot printers, chose to sacrifice his beliefs.

The fourth publication to appear in New Jersey was the *New-Jersey Gazette,* endorsed by the governor, subsidized by the legislature, and issued by the government printer.

No one seems to have been more concerned about New Jersey's fidelity to the patriot cause than the colony's first state governor, William Livingston. He was a temperamental Whig, a satiric orator, and, in John Adams's opinion, sensible, learned, and a ready writer.[11] Long before his move from New York to New Jersey in 1772, Livingston had established himself as an effective essayist and was, according to one literary historian, the principal poet that New York produced before the Revolution.[12]

Early evidence of Livingston's quixotic nature can be drawn from his first two "public" essays. The first, an indictment of the system of legal apprenticeships, appeared in Parker's *New-York Weekly Post-Boy* in August 1745. Less than a year later in the same newspaper he attacked his master's wife for excessive vanity and social pretentiousness. Both pieces were in reference to James Alexander, considered the dean of the New York bar and long-time friend of the prominent Livingston family. Young Livingston had been apprenticed to Alexander in 1741 after graduating from Yale, the most prominent of his class in terms of social position. The essays led to his dismissal from the law firm.

Livingston's most celebrated poem, entitled *Philosophic Solitude, or the Choice of a Rural Life,* was first published in New York in 1747 and reissued in 1762,

1769, 1782, and 1790. But his favorite literary form was the essay, and a number of his essays appeared in New York newspapers. In 1752 he was the principal promoter and editor of the short-lived *Independent Reflector,* as well as its chief contributor. A periodical of Whig liberalism, the *Reflector* was the first publication other than a regular newspaper in colonial New York. Its writers copied the style of the British *Independent Whig,* published by Thomas Gordon and John Trenchard, whose famous "Cato's Letters" remain outstanding today for their unusual and unqualified defense of libertarianism.

After having resided in New Jersey only a few years, Livingston was elected a delegate to the Continental Congress three consecutive times. He was called home in June 1776 to take command of the New Jersey militia at Elizabethtown. Then in August of that year he was elected governor of the new state in a close contest with Richard Stockton of Princeton. Almost immediately after his election Livingston set about in earnest to offset what he called "those amongst us who . . . are secretly abetting . . . to deprive us of that liberty, without which, man is a beast, and government a curse." He, of course, had to resort to out-of-state newspapers for his verbal campaign, in this case the *Pennsylvania Packet* of March 4, 1777. John Dunlap's newspaper, printed in Philadelphia, had emerged just prior to the war as an incalculably important medium for the patriots in the Middle Colonies.

Of particular annoyance to the new governor was Hugh Gaine's *New-York Gazette and Weekly Mercury* when it was issued from Newark. Gaine's paper had been the principal New York publication in opposition to the

Reflector, a sore point that had not healed during the twenty-year interim. "Who is the greatest liar upon earth?" asked a writer in William Bradford's *Pennsylvania Journal* on February 19, 1777. "Hugh Gaine, of New York, printer." Another patriot, writing in the *Gazette of the State of North Carolina* for April 9, accused Gaine of printing "pompous Accounts" of the "rapid Progress of the British Arms in America . . . calculated to delude an infatuated People." Editorial observations, often tinted with the Royalist argument, were frequent in Gaine's paper, but the printer usually denied all charges against him, retorting on one occasion that the Philadelphia newspapers were "stuffed with continued false accounts of Skirmishes and other Exploits of their Raggamuffins in the Jersies." [13]

Livingston, however, appeared to be disturbed not so much by Gaine and others who criticized the patriots as by the general lack of enthusiasm in New Jersey to fight for, as well as talk about, independence from Great Britain.

It is difficult to estimate how much of the newspaper debate was taken seriously by New Jerseyans. News and comment on political issues before the war, as with military issues during the war, were no doubt absorbed by those citizens who had access to newspapers and, more important, who could read. But even when literacy was a problem, people read to each other or spread the news by word of mouth—in the taverns, churches, and other centers of congregation. To combat what he believed to be the influence of the Tory press, Livingston wrote a long essay in February 1777 satirizing Gaine's style of journalism. Entitled the "Impartial Chronicle" in typical Livingston style, it appeared in the *Pennsylvania Packet*. Livingston sent a copy to General Washington and enclosed with it a brief letter of explanation. "The Impartial Chronicle is ridicule of Gaine's lying Gazette, which is a Jersey Production, and will probably afford you a little Diversion in a leisure moment." [14] Washington, evidently impressed, replied: "If Lucre [Lucifer] has a Spark of Modesty remaining, he must blush at seeing himself so vastly outdone in his ruling Passion." [15]

In their extensive correspondence Livingston and Washington dealt mainly with military affairs. In the spring of 1777 they were concerned with New Jersey's contemplated recruitment law. At Washington's encouragement Livingston fought for the passage of a strong law but settled for something less than he had hoped for. By July, Washington was aggravated and dismayed over military setbacks, but the commander was also worried about what he called the "pernicious tendency of falsehood and misrepresentation" in so-called news reports.

The general appealed to Congress for a "camp press." In a letter detailing the use of the press he said: "It would enable us to give speedy and exact information of any Military transactions that take place with proper comments upon them. If the People had a Channel of Intelligence, that from its usual authenticity they could look up to with confidence, they might often be preserved from that dispondency, which they are apt to fall into from the exaggerated pictures our Enemies and their emissaries among us commonly draw of any misfortunes we meet with." [16] What Washington seemed to regret most was the necessity to use distant Philadelphia newspapers, such as the *Pennsylvania Packet,* for dispatching military orders.

There is little reason to suppose that General Washington had only New Jersey in mind. His letter nonetheless reveals what he thought on the subject of public apathy and the dissemination of information at a time when his military forces depended a great deal upon the physical and moral support of New Jerseyans. Both Washington and Livingston had been thwarted in the spring of 1777 by a diluted militia law which first permitted the payment of money in lieu of actual military service and later allowed men to serve alternate months. In mid-1777 New Jersey's governor could not assure Washington the tactical support he needed following the British occupation of New York. Even so, as an experienced propagandist, Livingston could put the weight of his office behind a plan to disseminate reliable information and help bolster the spirits of citizens and soldiers alike.

The governor's efforts culminated in success in October and November 1777. The Assembly was meeting in Princeton, and in a message to this body on October 11 Livingston proposed that the state immediately subsidize the establishment of a weekly newspaper. "If at the End of six Months there shall be seven hundred or more Subscribers who will pay punctually," he said, "the Claim upon Government to cease. But if the Subscribers fall short of that Number, Government to become a Subscriber so as to make up that Number."

On November 5 the Assembly, which had been forced to evacuate Princeton and resume its session in Trenton, ordered a committee to take up the proposal with the state's public printer, Isaac Collins. The committee, made up of William Churchill Houston of Somerset County, Ephraim Harris of Cumberland County, and Samuel Rodgers of Burlington County, made its report the same day to the Assembly. They had found Collins "readily disposed . . . provided the Legislature will agree to give him some Encouragement and Assistance." For his part, Collins called for the *New-Jersey Gazette* to be printed weekly in four folio pages, the price to be twenty-six shillings a year, half to be paid at the time of subscribing and the rest at the end of the year. He accepted Livingston's suggestion for assuring at least seven hundred subscribers. Further, the printer requested that a "cross-post" system be worked out to expedite the delivery of papers from his printing office to the nearest post office, to be operated at the state's expense. This was not unusual, for it was common practice for post-riders to deliver newspapers along with the regular mail items. Finally, Collins wanted military exemptions for himself and four of his shop employees, "liable however to be taxed as other Exempts."

Houston, chairman of the committee, reported that his group was "clearly of the Opinion that a well-conducted Gazette would at any Time, but especially in the present Conjuncture, be of very essential Benefit to the good People of this State. The Enemy by their Emissaries, and the disaffected among ourselves, take all possible Pains to circulate, through the Country, their Papers and Handbills filled with the grossest Falsehoods and Misrepresentations, and purposely calculated to abuse and mislead the People, while we are without the least available

Means of defeating their mischievous Designs, by setting publick Events and Transactions in a true Point of View." Houston added that such a publication would "greatly tend to promote useful Knowledge and Arts in the State." [17] Next, Jacob Drake of Morris County and Kenneth Anderson of Monmouth County were directed to relay the Assembly's action to the Council. Concurrence came on November 6, and with it the birth of the *New-Jersey Gazette*. The first edition was pulled from Collins's press in Burlington on December 5, 1777, a little more than seven years after the printer had settled in New Jersey.

All of Collins's precautionary conditions were met. Moreover, in addition to exempting the printer and his workmen from military service, the Assembly and Council authorized a duplicate measure for the owner and two employees of William Shaffer's paper mill in Spotswood, not far from New Brunswick in Middlesex County. Shaffer had been under contract to supply paper to Collins since the mill was founded in 1776. Establishment of the cross-post, perhaps the most crucial condition, was also met. Collins's few extant records reveal that of the early riders, John Hedden and Alexander Anderson delivered the *Gazette* around the state and as far north as Essex County. In the beginning, each Assemblyman and Councilman served as a solicitor for the paper, thereby helping to guarantee the widest possible circulation in all counties.

Few, if any, colonial American periodicals were begun under such ideal conditions. Unfortunately, the official records do not reveal how much of an active role Collins took during the planning stages. The demise of numerous newspapers and magazines over the years probably served as a warning to him to be cautious. On the other hand, Collins could rather easily take on the publication of a weekly newspaper, once he had the additional equipment, since his other work already guaranteed the shop a substantial income. The main burden at the outset was the purchase of more equipment.

Even before he started printing the *Gazette,* the growth of Collins's business may have necessitated the installation of a second press and the purchase of several more fonts of type in assorted sizes; but in any case, he would have had to get a second press and more type in order to issue a weekly newspaper. Unlike pressmen, compositors worked continuously, and Collins had to have an ample supply of type in various sizes to spread among the jobs the shop was doing at any one time. To begin with, he would have needed a large amount of nonpareil, brevier, and bourgeois, the sizes, six, eight, and nine point in modern terms, used in newspaper printing. Since they were also used in most of the other products of his shop, Collins no doubt simply added to these basic sizes that he bought in 1770 and supplemented over the years.

Where he got type in 1777 we do not know, but by this time both Jacob Bay and Justus Fox were well-known founders in the neighborhood of Philadelphia. A resolution of the Pennsylvania Convention, dated January 23, 1775, reflects the policy against importation and in support of native manufactures: "Resolved unanimously, that as printing types are now made to a considerable degree of perfection by an ingenious artist in Germantown; it is recommended to the printers, to use such types in preference to any which may be hereafter imported." [18]

An inventory and appraisement taken in 1773 of the

late William Rind's shop in Williamsburg, where Collins served out his apprenticeship, provides data on the equipment in a typical two-press shop. In addition to long primer, English, and a small quantity of double pica, Rind stocked twenty-five pounds of a fairly new type, French canon, roughly the same as 48 point today and about the largest foundry type available in America at that time. He had two imposing stones on which type was locked into chases or galleys for printing. Rind owned fifteen chases, compared to the three pairs required in a one-press shop, and fifteen galleys, more than double the number Benjamin Franklin ordered some twenty years before for his New Haven shop. Besides a second press and more type, which in Rind's place required eighteen pairs of cases to store the various sizes, Collins had to increase his entire shop inventory to publish satisfactorily the *Gazette.* [19]

On the first page of the first number he published his "proposals," which amounted to "a brief Account of the Nature of his Plan." Apparently, Collins believed the general reader should know as soon as possible what to expect from the newspaper.

> To enter into a minute Detail of the Advantages of a well-conducted NEWS-PAPER, would, at any Time, be impertinent, but more especially at a Crisis which makes a quick Circulation of Intelligence particularly interesting to all the AMERICAN STATES. The Publisher therefore, thinks it will be more to the Purpose, to communicate to the Publick, a brief Account of the Nature of his Plan, than to enter into a formal Proof of it's Utility, which he esteems little less than self-evident.
>
> He proposes to print this GAZETTE once a Week, to contain a faithful Account of remarkable Occurrences

whether foreign or domestic: Materials for which he shall be amply furnished with, an Consequence of a general Correspondence he is establishing for that purpose.

Such Proceedings of the Legislature, and Courts of Justice as may conduce to the Benefit or Entertainment of his Readers, shall find a place in his Publication.

Essays, useful or entertaining, Schemes for the Advancement of TRADE, ARTS AND MANUFACTURES, Proposals for Improvements in AGRICULTURE and particularly in the Culure of HEMP and FLAX, will be inserted with Pleasure and Alacrity.

The Interests of RELIGION and LIBERTY, he will ever think it is his particular Duty to support; and at the same Time, to treat with disregard the intemperate Effusions of factious Zealots, whether religious or political, as injurious to Virtue, and destructive of Civil Order. With great Care shall he reject every Proposition to make his Paper a Vehicle for the dark Purposes of private malice, by propagating Calumnies against Individuals, wounding the Peace of Families, and inflaming the minds of men with Bitterness and Rancour against one another.

In a Word, he will spare neither Cost or Pains to make his Paper as useful and entertaining as possible; and while these Objects are steadily pursued, the Publisher will confidently rely upon the Generosity and Publick Spirit of the Gentlemen of this State, for their Countenance and Support, to such a useful Undertaking.[20]

How effective Collins and his *Gazette* were in rallying New Jerseyans to give more support to the war is impossible to determine. The victories at Trenton and Princeton the year before had, in the words of one historian, "entirely altered the military balance in New Jersey." [21] Nevertheless, the war was to last much longer, and New Jersey was almost constantly a theater of British raids.

From the first number of the *Gazette* it carried news of the war, and Governor Livingston used it as a regular medium on communications. On several occasions he exhorted the militia "to turn out with alacrity, at a time when Providence seems to have presented you with a glorious opportunity for defeating the common enemy." The newspaper regularly carried such calls to arms notices from Washington as well as from Livingston. From his encampment at Valley Forge during the winter of 1777–78, Washington wrote New Jersey's governor: "I cannot but be highly sensible of the fresh proofs given, of that zeal which yourself in particular, and the State of New Jersey in general, have so uniformly manifested in the common cause, and of the polite regard you have in repeated instances shown of my applications." [22]

Although the *Gazette* was unique among eighteenth-century periodicals in that it was founded and edited almost exclusively for the patriot cause in New Jersey, it was not particularly unusual in other ways. Its name, for example, was the most common of the early newspaper titles. Its four pages, printed on both sides of two 16 x 20-inch folio leaves, measured half that size, or 10 x 16 inches, and were called small folio. Its customary three columns offered news items of general interest clipped from American and foreign papers together with an abundance of local material such as essays, letters, and poems. The type of material printed depended upon what the editor believed to be of interest to his readers. Citizens, for instance, thirsted for European tidings and news from other colonies, but they showed only slight interest in local affairs. They were likely to hear of nearby events as soon as the editor did; moreover, interest often faded before most local stories could be published in the weekly chronicle.

Advertisements, which were supposed to pay for the cost of printing the paper, received nearly equal attention with news. In addition to the many advertisements of items for sale by local merchants, paid notices appeared regularly, advertising for strayed livestock and runaway slaves. "It is the advertiser who provides the paper for the subscriber," wrote the publisher of the *New York Evening Post* in 1803. Noah Webster put it more explicitly in 1798, when he said: "A literary paper without advertisements would cost fifteen or twenty dollars a year, if daily, & in proportion, if published once or twice a week." [23]

The frequency of the *Gazette*'s publication (each Wednesday) greatly increased Collins's problems of labor and paper. Almost immediately the additional work load necessitated taking on another apprentice. On December 10, 1777, the second week of publication, Collins advertised for "a lad about 14 years of age, who can read, and write a fair hand, and can be well recommended for his honesty and sobriety." Many times during the years Collins issued the *Gazette* he sought apprentices and journeyman printers and pressmen. Wages for printers were comparatively high. In Philadelphia printers commanded as much as £100 currency (£60 sterling) "found" —that is, when the worker was given food or lodging. Carpenters, by contrast, could expect from £45 to £90 sterling, not found, or £30 to £60 found. "Scattered sources indicate that most artisans could expect from £25 to £30 sterling found or £40 to £45 not found, though poor ones were paid as little as £20 not found and first-rate men received as much as £50 sterling found." [24] If, indeed, Collins could always have hired the workmen he needed, a major undertaking in itself, he would have been forced to pay handsomely. However, master printers were among the eighteenth-century's wealthiest entrepreneurs.

The printer's paper supply was an equally serious problem. Paper, made by hand from rags, preferably linen, had to be imported from Great Britain until domestic mills were started. By 1777, however, Collins could buy his stock from several mills in nearby Pennsylvania and in New Jersey. But since the mills were wholly dependent upon available rags, they were almost always behind the expanding printing trade. So great was the problem that it was common practice for newspapers to be late in delivery or suspended outright, as the publisher put it, "for want of Paper." Nearly each week in the *Gazette* Collins printed this appeal: "A GOOD PRICE AND READY MONEY Is given by the Printer hereof, for CLEAN LINEN RAGS."

After thirteen numbers of the *Gazette* had been issued from Burlington, Collins moved his family and equipment up the river to the larger and more prominent city of Trenton in February 1778. Because of its strategic location at the head of navigation on the Delaware, Trenton had become a transfer point for wheat, iron, and lumber of the upper Delaware Valley destined for shipment down the river to Philadelphia. Moreover, important stage lines between Philadelphia and New York crossed the ferry at Trenton. Also, the city was assured industrial activity because of its abundance of water power and its location in the midst of a region of rich natural resources.[25]

Peter Kalm, the Swedish traveler, in 1748 found Trenton's wealth the result of its thriving river trade, including passengers as well as goods. The inhabitants' "chief gain consisted in the arrival of the numerous travellers between that city [Philadelphia] and New York; for they are commonly brought by the Trenton Yachts from Philadelphia to Trenton, or from thence to Philadelphia. But from Trenton, further to New Brunswick, the travellers go in wagons, which set out every day for that place. Several of the inhabitants also subsist on the carriage of all sorts of goods, which are sent in great quantities, either from Philadelphia to New York, or from thence to the former place—for between Philadelphia and Trenton, all goods go by water; but between Trenton and New Brunswick, they are all carried by land, and both these conveniences belong to people of this town." [26]

Despite relocation in a larger shop in a larger town, and despite the *Gazette*'s rising circulation, the printer announced in April of that year that "no more Subscriptions can be received at present . . . for Want of Paper." This was an old story, to be repeated often by Collins and contemporary printers. He appealed to every family in New Jersey to save their rags and to send them either to William Shaffer's paper mill in Spotswood, or to Anthony Armbruster's new mill in Burlington, or even to the printing office. Collins offered threepence a pound for "those that are delivered clean whether coarse or fine, or whether Cotton or Linen." Shopkeepers were also asked to cooperate, "to Whom a Compensation will be made."

Beset with these problems, Collins pressed for a legislative measure which would alleviate the scarcity of paper. In March 1778 he petitioned both governmental houses to assist Stacy Potts, a Quaker businessman who happened to be a distant relative of the printer's wife, in establishing a paper mill in Trenton. Such help had been given to Shaffer when the *Gazette* was still in the planning stage. Shaffer regularly shipped supplies of paper to Collins, as agreed. But a mill closer to the printing shop would be valuable and, conceivably, more dependable. Collins thus urged the legislature to support the Potts enterprise.[27]

In his petition to the lawmakers Collins warned that paper had become very scarce, "dear and difficult to be had." "There is Reason to fear," he added, "without some publick Encouragement is given for manufacturing it, in a short Time a sufficient Quantity cannot be procured at any Rate." The legislators must have wondered about the Shaffer mill, for it had only been a few months since Collins had persuaded them to give preferential treatment to the Spotswood firm. Collins responded that the mill had not lived up to expectations, "and for what little he is capable of furnishing, he [Shaffer] charges extravagant Prices." On the other hand, the printer said, Potts was better qualified and prepared to open a mill, provided the legislature passed an act to exempt the owner and several of his hands, not to exceed five, from service in the militia.

The bill to support Potts got through the Council, but failed in the lower house. The Assembly approved instead a more universal act that spelled out exemptions "at each and every [paper] Mill or Works, erected or to be erected and carried on in this State." Thus in the end Collins got his "publick Encouragement," although not exclusively for Potts. The bill became law on June 20, 1778.

Another development in Trenton helped make it possible for Potts to proceed with his original plan to open a paper mill. John Reynolds, an experienced Germantown papermaker who, two years before, had also been unsuccessful in winning legislative support for a mill in New Jersey, moved to Trenton and awaited the outcome of Collins's lobbying efforts for Potts. In December 1778 the new partnership of Potts and Reynolds was publicly announced in the *Gazette*. The partners reported that their Trenton mill was nearly completed and urged New Jersey inhabitants to save rags. They advertised again in the next month, appealing to the mothers of school-age children, "the present great scarcity of that useful article, without which their going to school would avail them but little." They said they hoped to remedy the paper problem shortly.

Two years later Potts and Reynolds again advertised in the *Gazette,* on March 28, 1781. The mill probably began to furnish Collins with paper about the spring of 1779, but there is no record of how long it continued to operate.

Besides the difficulty in securing paper, the lack of public support contributed greatly to the mortality rate among newspapers. Despite the *Gazette*'s government subsidy in the beginning, Collins was always plagued with debts because of subscribers who were in arrears. On November 25, 1778, for example, the publisher, in urging his subscribers to settle their accounts, reminded them that the price of the *Gazette,* twenty-six shillings a year, was less than that of papers in neighboring states. By then the government's six-month obligation had ceased, and Collins said that in order to continue publication he would have to increase the price to two dollars a quarter, or more than double the original annual rate in British currency.[28]

Next, Collins devised a plan whereby persons who subscribed to twelve issues would receive a bonus of two additional issues free, providing, of course, they were punctual in making remittances. "If this mode can be carried into practice," he agreed "to lower the price of the *Gazette* to a *Dollar* and a *Half* by the quarter. By this means the Paper may be carried on without loss, and the State served by a repository of Intelligence and useful Knowledge highly interesting to all." Even then, the *Gazette* was expensive to buy *and* to produce.

Collins tried to increase the *Gazette*'s circulation by adding to the number of agents, or "packetmakers," as they were called, who distributed the paper. Philadelphians, for example, could buy the *Gazette* at Moses Bartram's apothecary on Second Street near Arch Street and from Robert Aitken, the bookbinder and publisher, on Front Street. Collins's former partner, Joseph Crukshank, also carried the paper. All, it is interesting to note, were personal friends of the *Gazette*'s publisher. Subscription worries continued, however.

Nearly every issue of the *Gazette* throughout the spring of 1779 carried polite appeals, stern warnings, and even caustic threats. By June, Collins confessed to his readers that he had been "a very considerable Loser, owing to the Depreciation of the Money, the increased Price of Wages and every Article used in the Printing Business." Forced, as he put it, "to fall upon some Plan for fixing the Value of Subscriptions," he suggested a barter system that would enable subscribers to keep up with payments. Thus, in place of money, the publisher agreed to accept produce, such as wheat, rye, buckwheat, corn, wool, flax, butter, and cheese, "Those Gentlemen who are not in the farming Way, to pay Cash in Proportion." This system was a rather common mercantile practice in the eighteenth century during the recurring periods of economic stress.

Adding to the problems of the publisher of the *Gazette*, there appeared in February 1779 a rival New Jersey newspaper. Until then Collins's only competition had come from outside the state. The publisher of the *New-Jersey Journal,* printed in Chatham in the north-central part of the state, was Shepard Kollock, a long-time friend of Collins's who had been released from active military duty to start another patriot paper in the north to help offset Tory propaganda. With the occupation of New York by the British, the Whigs found themselves faced not only with Hugh Gaine's ambivalent publication and the triumphant return of James Rivington but also with two more Royalist journals. Rivington resumed his attack on the patriots in 1777 with the establishment of his *Royal Gazette.* James and Alexander Robertson had been encouraged by the British to begin their *Royal American Gazette,* and in 1779 William Lewis started his *Mercury.*

Immediately after the first copy of the *Journal* reached Collins, he sought to renew Governor Livingston's confidence in the *Gazette.* In response, Livingston assured the publisher that "the blaze of our *Eastern Comet* 'The New Jersey Journal' has not diverted my attention from the western light, the Gazette which I heartily wish will continue to shine its primitive lustre." [29] Livingston said he thought the *Journal* would "shortly go out like a meteor, while the other luminary increases in strength and splendor." He said he felt bound to patronize the *Gazette;* after all, he helped establish it as the "official" state paper. However, had Collins been sufficiently discouraged at that time by the many problems of newspaper publishing, he could have used the arrival of a second patriot paper in the state as an excuse for terminating the *Gazette*. New Jersey, which had had no established newspaper until Collins's, now had two, and the Trenton publisher could have reasoned that the death of one would still not leave the state without its own medium of news. But he did not make such a decision.

The *Journal* was issued from Chatham until 1783. Kollock then moved on to New Brunswick to publish another paper before resuming publication of the *Journal* in 1785 in Elizabethtown. It is interesting that two former employees of William Goddard's, Collins and Kollock, were the publishers of New Jersey's first two established newspapers. Since Kollock's *Journal* received support from the army and Collins's *Gazette* from the state, New Jersey's first newspapers were conceived at the instance of the government of the new nation.[30]

However many subscribers—or potential ones—the *Journal* in the east may have coaxed away from the *Gazette* in the west, delinquent payments finally forced Collins to suspend publication for three weeks in July 1779. He apologized publicly for the drastic measure, but said that he had not received much more than half the amount of the subscriptions for 1778 and "not near the whole for the last six months." He reminded his readers that he had undertaken publication of the *Gazette* "at the pressing instance of many Gentlemen of leading character in the State." He said he had continued the paper "even to the manifest prejudice of his own fortune, well convinced of how great utility such a publication might be to the interests of Religion, Liberty, and Science." He reaffirmed his willingness "to be subservient to this great object as far as his ability will admit if consistent with the means of living." Collins guaranteed subscribers the return of their money if the publication were discontinued. Meeting with some success, he did not again have to suspend publication until four years later.

In the meantime, a personal complication occurred in 1778. The "manifest prejudice of his own fortune," to which the printer had referred his subscribers the previous July, probably alluded partly to Collins's disownment by the Society of Friends. As official printer to a "revolutionary" government and publisher of a patriot newspaper, he had committed himself "hearty in the American cause," the phrase he had used to recommend Kollock for a military post. Unlike many Quakers, Collins subscribed to the ideals of public justice and self-defense, as he put it, that often ran counter to the Quaker peaceable testimony. Even though he did not literally serve in the militia, he had agreed to be exempted to publish a newspaper, a decision tantamount in the Quaker view to military service.

On May 4, 1778, the Burlington Monthly Meeting heard a report that Collins "hath transgressed the Rules of our Discipline, by paying in Effect, his Fine in lieu of Personal service in the militia . . . for which he had been treated with divers Times but hath not cleared himself thereof to satisfaction." [31] The overseers named to confront Collins were David Ridgway, Aaron Wills, George Dillwyn, and Samuel Allinson. Although the procedure was a routine Quaker measure, it must have been particularly difficult for Dillwyn and Allinson, who were close friends of Collins. They were required to present Collins with the charge against him and to report his response at the next meeting.

Collins considered the charge, and at the June 1 session the overseers reported that the printer "expressed his Sorrow thereupon, and seemed desirous of a little more time for Consideration." During the month Collins doubtless reexamined a number of his personal tenets, both spiritual and temporal. Fully aware of his Quaker heritage, an asset in West Jersey, the legislature had appointed him government printer in 1770. The state government had asked him seven years later to publish New Jersey's first, and, by patriot standards, greatly needed weekly newspaper. For financial reasons, quite apart from any moral obligation, the course he would take was obvious. He had gone too far to turn back, both as a wise and frugal businessman and as a wise and devoted public servant.

At the August Monthly Meeting two of the overseers reported that they had again called on the printer in late July. They said that Collins "differed from Friends in some Points, and if they thought his conduct repugnant to the Rules of Society they might proceed against him." Disownment proceedings were drawn up and read at the

September 7 meeting. Ridgway and Allinson delivered a copy to Collins, reminding him of his right to appeal. He refused and in so doing remained an outsider for nearly ten years. The action did not reflect on members of his family, for his wife and five children were admitted to the Chesterfield Meeting near Trenton.

❧ IV ❧
NEWSPAPER
EDITOR

Protests from "those persons who are ever ready to censure" greeted the first number of the *New-Jersey Gazette* on December 5, 1777. Having described the nature of the problem to Governor Livingston, Collins went on to say: "He who undertakes to print a News-Paper at any Time, and more especially at the present, need not expect to escape it, however well he may have meant." [1] Collins alluded to an article he had carried under the paper's regular London heading that was believed by some readers to be harmful to the patriot cause. In part the article reported that England had signed a pact with Russia and Prussia, "that the army in America, next campaign," reinforced by soldiers from these countries, "will not be short of 80,000." There were patriots who thought Collins should be reprimanded for printing what must surely be an untrue statement. The editor of the *Gazette* held a different view.

"I conceived the Publick were so well aware of the Enemy's Disingenuousness in their Accounts," he said in the same letter to Livingston, "that I apprehended the publishing of *such* would rather tend to place them in their proper ridiculous Point of Light, than having had an effect on the well-affected among us." Since the Tories had little trouble in spreading these false accounts, Collins said he thought it would be better generally to publish them with animadversions, or, after they are published, "totally contradict them." His first attempt at objective journalism, albeit politically naïve, apparently backfired. Collins desired to fight propaganda with truth, but instead learned his first lesson in editing a newspaper during a national emergency. Faithful to his intention, however, he printed in the second number of the *Gazette* on December 10 an extract from a letter which reported that the king of Prussia was still friendly toward the American patriots, and he offered more confirmation the following week.

Also in the *Gazette* for December 10 Collins reported under the regular Burlington heading that on the previous Thursday night the British army, which had occupied Philadelphia since late in September, had begun to march out of the town. "By Friday morning the whole had got as far as Chestnut-Hill, above German-town, in order to attack General Washington," whose army was posted nearby at Whitemarsh. "In consequence whereof," the report continued, "several skirmishes have happened between the pickets of the two armies. On Sunday Colonel Morgan's riflemen fell in with a large column of the enemy, near Jenkin's Town, on the Old York road, when a smart engagement ensued. A very heavy fire was kept up from about ten o'clock in the morning till twelve. At one they began again, and sustained the whole fire from the enemy's column till three in the afternoon, when it ceased for near an hour; and about four a slight firing commenced, which continued till sunset."

In this typical newspaper dispatch, which Collins probably received from a person who had seen the fighting, the editor recorded "about twenty men killed and wounded; among the latter is Major Morris, a brave and good officer, who is like to do well." As *Gazette* readers later found out, the Americans took up winter quarters at Valley Forge, twenty miles away, leaving the British, under General William Howe, in possession of Philadelphia.

Collins, as editor of the *Gazette,* usually tried to piece together in the same stories distant news about the war and news of actual fighting in and around New Jersey. Following the December 10 story on the skirmishes near Philadelphia, he attempted to inform his readers on developments in London. From the *London Gazette* of August 22, 1777, he extracted parts of a letter from General Howe to Lord George Germain, a member of the British supreme command, dated July 5, 1777, regarding troop movements and suggestions for the defense of Perth Amboy. Although such reports always reached *Gazette* readers long after the fact, Collins was doing what he could to provide "a faithful Account of remarkable Occurrences whether foreign or domestic."

He also announced that the "PIECE *signed* HORTEN-TIUS, *is come to hand, and will be inserted in our next.*"

This marked the beginning of Governor Livingston's long series of essays, written under that pseudonym presumably to avoid confusion between his official proclamations as governor, which appeared regularly in the *Gazette,* and his personal tirades, some of which were leveled against legislators.

In Livingston's first *Gazette* article as "Hortentius," he dealt with the first London dispatch. "According to custom," he wrote in the issue for December 17, "the new lie (that is the old lie reiterated) for next summer is, that we are to be devoured bones and all, by 36,000 Russians; besides something or other that is to be done to us by the King of Prussia." In his famous satirical style, he went on to ridicule, perhaps at Collins's suggestion, this most recent example of British propaganda.

"Hortentius" then proposed the exchange of General John Burgoyne," who had been captured following his army's defeat at Saratoga in October, "in such manner as will at the same time flatter his vanity, and redound to the greatest emolument of America." He further proposed that officers of like rank be exchanged: a general for a general, a colonel for a colonel, and so forth. And since Burgoyne possessed more offices, or more titles, "than any Gentleman on this side the *Ganges,*" Livingston opined that he was worth about several persons in exchange: one esquire, two major generals, three colonels of light horse, two governors, one member of Congress, the admiral of the navy, one commander-in-chief in a separate department, and six privates.

However diverted Collins may have been by Livingston's humor, he nonetheless quickly learned that partisan feelings were not to be taken lightly. Tempers flared easily. Those who had objected to the London story had not forgotten that the *Gazette,* a state-supported enterprise, had been established to help contradict the antirepublican influence of the Tory press. Although the British government had restrained the colonial press prior to the war, freedom of the press during Collins's years as an editor was threatened not so much by the British as it was by the Sons of Liberty and other Whig extremist groups like the one that sacked James Rivingston's shop in New York in 1775.

This brief clash, the first of several that Collins experienced as a newspaper editor, points up the fact that freedom of speech, an independent concept of personal liberty particularly important to a Quaker's theory of equality, was generally a late development in America. As one constitutional historian, Leonard W. Levy, writes: "The American people simply did not understand that freedom of thought and expression means equal freedom for the other fellow, especially the one with hated ideas." [2]

Besides another "Hortentius" piece, the *Gazette* for December 24, 1777, contained a legislative act for procuring "certain Articles of Clothing for the Use of the New-Jersey Regiments on the Continental Establishment," passed in Princeton on November 25 and signed by John Hart, the Assembly speaker. Another act called for the regulation and limitation of prices of certain critical commodities, an effort to curb wartime inflation and thus the depreciation of currency. The *Gazette* reported the appointment of John Witherspoon, Abraham Clark, Jonathan Elmer, Nathaniel Scudder, and Elias Boudinot as New Jersey delegates to the Continental Congress.

The Burlington column contained a message from General Washington's headquarters near Philadelphia, in which the commander-in-chief expressed his appreciation to the New Jersey officers and soldiers "for the fortitude and patience with which they have sustained the fatigues of the campaign." This was in reference to the encounter with Howe's forces on the outskirts of Philadelphia in the early part of the month. Collins reported in the same column that three New Jersey commissioners had been appointed to attend a convention in New Haven on January 15 "to form a plan of general regulation respecting the limiting prices of sundry articles of produce, manufacture and trade."

Collins personally announced that the Burlington almanac for 1778 was "in the Press, and speedily will be Published." He advertised for clean linen rags to be used in the making of paper and cited the prices for advertising in the *Gazette*—those of "moderate length" inserted for seven shillings and sixpence the first week, two shillings sixpence thereafter, and "long ones in Proportion."

Besides serving as a week-to-week medium of topical news, the *Gazette* helped to circulate the text of important documents. In the issue for January 7, 1778, Collins reported that the long-awaited "Articles of Confederation and Perpetual Union," in effect the nation's first constitution, had been published by Congress and sent to the states for ratification. The text did not appear in the *Gazette* until April 29; however, New Jersey citizens could read them two months before they were presented for formal acceptance by the states. In other states they were available only in pamphlet form.

Meanwhile, General Washington, writing from Valley

Forge on December 20, 1777, had used Collins's paper to "require all persons residing within seventy miles of Headquarters thresh one half of their grain by the first day of February and other half by first of March." The severe food and clothing problems of the Continentals require no further comment here.

The *Gazette* acted, too, as a kind of public guardian. On January 14, 1778, Collins warned the public of counterfeit $30 bills circulating in the area of Burlington. "They are dated May 10, 1775, done on copper-plate, and easily discovered." He said that on the back of the genuine bill the word Philadelphia was spelled *Philadelpkia,* and that of the counterfeit properly. "The figure of the lower ship in the true bill, especially its bottom, is much blacker and less discernable than in the counterfeit; and the paper of the latter is much thinner and smoother. And in that of the counterfeit in the upper *ship* a ray of light appears between *it* and the representation of the sea, which is not so in the genuine bill." The states' habit of printing large quantities of paper currency, itself no cure for inflation, made it rather easy for counterfeiters to circulate the fake variety. Collins had printed currency for his state, but his bills were said to be difficult, if not impossible, to copy.

Collins found himself again in editorial difficulties a year after the episode about the Russian troops. This time the center of controversy was the recently deposed General Charles Lee. In the *Gazette* for December 31, 1778, the editor inserted an allegorical essay about a mercenary soldier, which had originally appeared in the *Virginia Gazette* in 1775. As preface to the article, Collins had printed a letter from "A.B.," which said in part: "The attempt of a certain General officer lately condemned by a Court-martial for his malconduct, to raise a party in his favour, by calling in question the abilities not only of our illustrious Commander in Chief, but that of all our General officers—has justly raised the indignation of every honest man. His publications are an insult to America."

Soon after being suspended from service for his ignominious role in the Battle of Monmouth in June 1778 Lee took to writing in his own defense, and produced a lengthy statement which first appeared in the *Pennsylvania Packet,* a Whig newspaper, for December 3 and was reprinted five days later in William Goddard's *Maryland Journal.* The letter Collins printed referred to this statement by the embittered Lee. Neither the letter nor the article that followed mentioned Lee by name, but Lee was enraged by the obvious allusion. He wrote of his discontent to Governor Livingston, thinking that the state's chief executive would take action against the state's printer. The governor, however, attempted to smooth over the matter by weighing all sides of the argument.

"I can assure you," Livingston wrote Lee, "that I cannot but disapprove of Mr. Collins's inserting the paper you refer to in his Gazette. But I must declare in justice to him & from what I personally know is his humane disposition & his disinclination to convey through the channel of his Press any thing injurious to the reputation of others that I firmly believe he has taken the paper presentation as a copy of a publication in Virginia as a true copy." What Collins had presented to the New Jersey public as "a mere republication of a paper formerly printed by a Virginian Tory" had been, according to Lee, reprinted with "many alterations & additions." Though the tone of Livingston's letter to Lee is apologetic, it pointed out that "a printer by the bare republication of a paper is not presumed to adopt the sentiments" of the author. "But I should however be very sorry to find any of our printers imitating the practice of the British Subjects in New York, who whether they exceed us in military discipline & courage or not have to my certain knowledge hitherto surpassed us in printed calumny & detraction." Livingston did, however, criticize Lee for the officer's "reported" endeavors "to lessen the estimation in which G. Washington is held by the most virtuous Citizens of America." [3]

Collins reciprocated by publishing in the issue for January 27 a letter in behalf of Lee which answered the "scandalous libel" of the original item. Collins and Livingston probably consulted each other during the controversy, for the records show that they maintained a running correspondence. James Rivington, the New York Tory editor, once called Collins "Mr. Livingston's Printer," presumably in anger over the well-lubricated Collins-Livingston propaganda device which frequently exposed, in their view, Rivington's accounts of the war as "the fertility of the *royal* Printer's invention." [4] Collins himself was admonished in a letter in the *Gazette* for March 24 to be more careful in reporting and editing the news, "for as you are a Whig they know the truth of the publication would not be questioned."

Of the *Gazette*'s contents, none are more interesting reading today than the letters addressed "To the Printer," or to "Mr. Collins." Unlike the present-day "Voice of the

People" columns, these highly personal essays were seldom brief and were often continued over several issues of the paper. Since the life of the *Gazette* covered approximately the duration of the Revolutionary War and the first critical years of the new national government, these letter-writers were concerned with military battles and political events.

Not all of the editor's correspondence got into print. Collins occasionally rejected a letter, sometimes with a printed explanation in the *Gazette*. One such item, sent to him from "A Farmer's Daughter," was refused as "too incorrect for publication," a cryptic reply that must have titillated the imaginations of some newspaper readers. As editor, Collins also fancied himself as a literary critic; he rejected a letter from "Old Soldier," and recommended certain revisions "so that it may go forth in a deserved dress."

The first installment of one of the long reader discourses started on the first page of the *Gazette* for March 17, 1779. The author, "True Patriot," dismayed over the way national affairs were going, charged that some "malignant disorder has seized upon our body politic, and threatens at least an interruption of our advances to manhood, if not a political dissolution." He bemoaned the decay of public spirit, the unequal division of property, and the general loss of social virtues. In the second installment, he outlined the causes of these national evils and their remedies. By the time the fourth installment was published, Collins had begun to receive correspondence from other disturbed readers. One, an assistant purchasing agent for New Jersey, Azariah Dunham of Morristown, criticized "True Patriot" for his vilification of military commissaries, and "the whole host of their deputies," of which Dunham was one. Dunham denied all the charges. "Timoleon," meanwhile, turned the debate into a three-way affair. He accused Dunham of having bought and sold supplies for the army at advanced prices for his private emolument. Dunham retorted: "Neither the scorching heats of summer, the cold rigors of winter, the severity of tempests nor the darkness of the night, have repressed my endeavours . . . to obtain proper supplies for the army." One can understand Collins's decision to discontinue such topical, but entertaining, debates, which soon degenerated into personal assaults. Deciding when to cut them off was the editor's weekly responsibility.

Another test of Collins's editorial principles came in October 1779, when the upper house of the state legislature registered a complaint against a satirical article by "Cincinnatus." Upset over what amounted to an anonymous attack on Governor Livingston and the College of New Jersey (now Princeton), the Council demanded of Collins the true name of the author. The Council professed the belief that "the Freedom of the Press ought to be tolerated as far as it is consistent with the Good of the People, and the Security of the Government established under their Authority." Ironically, the Americans interpreted the common law of seditious libel much as the British had. On October 28 the Council resolved that the *Gazette*'s editor should be forced to reveal the author's name. Collins refused. He was supported in his stand by a seventeen to eleven vote in the Assembly, which thereby set an early legal precedent for freedom of the press in New Jersey.[5]

95

Collins stated his reason for not disclosing the author's identity in a letter to the Council dated October 30. He said: "Were I to comply with the requisition contained in this resolution, without the permission of the author of the piece alluded to, I conceive I should betray the trust reposed in me, and be far from acting as a faithful guardian of the Liberty of the Press." [6]

Elsewhere printers had similar problems with legislative attempts to suppress their newspapers. For example, John Dunlap, publisher of the *Pennsylvania Packet*, received an order from delegates to the Continental Congress in January 1779 to appear before them and reveal the name of the author of an offensive "Common Sense" letter in the *Packet*. In this case, however, the printer decided to identify Thomas Paine, who had written that France had been providing secret aid to the American revolutionists before the Franco-American Alliance became official. Dunlap temporarily lost his job as printer of the *Journals of Congress* and Paine was forced to resign his post as secretary to the Committee on Foreign Affairs. Later on, Dunlap got into another wrangle when he published a pseudonymous attack on members of Congress written by Dr. Benjamin Rush, but this time neither the printer nor the author was called to answer for his insolence. [7]

Despite Collins's position on the matter, Governor Livingston interrupted his writing as "Hortentius" in 1780. His decision may not have stemmed from the "Cincinnatus" affair, intended to prejudice the legislature against his reelection as governor. Some legislators earlier had expressed dissatisfaction with the governor's extracurricular writing. "With respect to the late silence of Hortentius," Livingston wrote Collins, "would you believe that among the weighty charges exhibited against me at the joint meeting to prevent my reelection . . . one was that I had published pieces in your papers under the signature of Hortentius. I am sorry that the objection was made by one of the friends, tho' I dont suppose that the friends are answerable either for his malice or his nonsense." [8] Though there is no reason to believe that Livingston held Collins, who was also a Quaker, responsible in any way for the attempt to unseat him, the printer felt impelled to explain his own position on such matters.

"Time was," Collins recollected in a long letter to Livingston, "when I felt myself obliged as a Citizen by your Friendship and Acquaintance. I flattered myself that I had your entire Approbation and good Wishes in my Profession. As Publisher of the *New-Jersey Gazette,* I could not but be highly sensible of the Advantages it derived from your Encouragement, Attention, and Support." [9] Collins was noticeably disturbed over what he called in Livingston an "Alteration of Conduct." He then alluded to an unfortunate article which "drew after it Consequences," and went on to delineate his best defense of press freedom in an effort, as he put it, to do away with every cause of "Estrangement and Disgust."

"My Ear is open to every Man's Instruction but to no Man's influences," Collins declared, underlining each word. So far as he had been capable of comprehending the nature of press freedom, he said he had maintained a "Sovereign Respect" for it. "If I have at any Time, been mistaken in this Respect, those who know me best will most readily declare that I have waited only for Correction to alter what was wrong. Difference of opinion is a

common Thing, but I deny and scorn the Imputation of being wilfully in Error." Since 1777, the year Collins began the *Gazette,* he had faced enough criticism to inspire him to write a "position paper."

He had been accused from time to time of conspiring with writers whose motives were thought to be of a questionable patriotic nature. But he held to a position that we now take for granted, that the opinions of writers are not necessarily those held by a journal's editor. Collins also affirmed to his governor that he was neither disaffected nor indifferent to the interests of his country. He said: "No personal Dislike or Disrespect had any share in my Conduct. My whole Behavior is, and ever has been, a direct Contradiction to every Thing of this kind." In appealing to Livingston's own respect for free expression, Collins said he felt compelled to explain his views on the editing of a journal of fact and opinion, "as one who is desirous of being useful to the Cause of Liberty and Virtue." To make his position clear once and for all, he said he would never decline any means of removing "a subsisting Uneasiness and Misunderstanding," provided that they were not "unworthy of an independent Citizen conscious of having done intentional Injury to no man." With this, the editor of the *New-Jersey Gazette* laid some claim to civil liberty at a time in American history when "liberty of speech belonged solely to those who spoke the speech of liberty." [10]

During such recurring threats to his freedom as editor, Collins usually drew upon traditional libertarian views to convince his subscribers, if not some legislators and other powerful townspeople, that freedom to speak required a constant struggle. Soon after he wrote his defense of press freedom in the letter to Livingston, there appeared on the last page of the *Gazette* for June 6, 1781, this poem, *"Said to be written by* DR. FRANKLIN*,"* entitled *"On the* FREEDOM *of the* PRESS*"*:

> While free from force the Press remains,
> Virtue and freedom chear our plains,
> And learning largesses bestows,
> And keeps *unlicens'd open house.*
> We to the nation's publick mart,
> Our works of wit, and schemes of art,
> And philosophic goods this way,
> Like water-carriage, cheap convey.
> This *tree* which knowledge so affords,
> *Inquisitors* with flaming swords
> From *lay-approach* with zeal defend,
> Lest *their own* paradise should end.
> The Press from her foecundous womb,
> Brought forth the arts of Greece and Rome;
> Her off'spring, skill'd in logic war,
> Truth's banner wav'd in open air;
> And lawless pow'r, the long kept field,
> By reason quell'd, was forc'd to yield.
> This *Nurse of arts,* and *Freedom's fence,*
> To chain is treason against sense;
> And liberty, thy thousand tongues,
> None silence who design no wrongs;
> For those that use the gag's restraint,
> First rob, before they stop complaint.

In reporting developments of the war and other timely news Collins was of course hampered by slow communications, but news items appeared in the paper shortly after they reached his office. The time lag was not between receipt of news and publication, but rather between the news event itself and the date Collins received his information from either a military courier or an ordinary citizen. However, geographical proximity was always a factor, as was the case in 1778 when a British expedition of armed vessels and flat-bottomed boats invaded nearby Bordentown a few months after the printer had moved to Trenton. The expedition headed up the Delaware to Trenton, only to be repulsed by the local militia. A few weeks later a large force of British and Hessian soldiers, having vacated Philadelphia, started moving across New Jersey to New York. A small party of Continentals managed to check their advance toward Trenton, but several troops got close enough to frighten the townspeople. Collins, aware of the event but also convinced that it would not be news by the time it reached print, reported it in the *Gazette* for July 1 in this way: "The near approach of the enemy prevented the publication of this paper last week." He had intended to print his edition for June 24, but had to stop when the soldiers threatened the town the day before. The Collins printers sought temporary safety, as did the rest of Trenton's inhabitants.

Conversely, a special supplement, called in those days an "extraordinary," to the *Gazette* of July 8, 1778, was given over entirely to a letter from General Washington to the president of Congress, describing in detail the Battle of Monmouth on June 28.

Although Collins seems to have reported news as quickly and accurately as possible, it is of interest to the student of journalism that the New Jersey printer ignored what history has recorded as one of the biggest events of Trenton's early years. On July 27, 1786, one of the first boats in America to be propelled by steam traversed the Delaware near Trenton, but neither the event nor word of the boat's inventor, John Fitch, was reported in the *Gazette*. Collins knew of Fitch's invention and his troubles in getting financial help from Congress. As government printer, Collins must have been aware of New Jersey's decision in 1786 to give Fitch exclusive right for fourteen years to construct, employ, and navigate steamboats.[11] Collins probably reasoned that the incident, like the British approach to Trenton in 1778, would be common knowledge before the next edition of the *Gazette*.

News from distant points was likely to receive fuller coverage. In the *Gazette* of May 31, 1784, the editor wrote: "Our desire to gratify, as early as possible, the publick curiosity concerning the experiments of Messrs. Charles and Robert, with the Air Balloon, December 1, 1783, hath induced us to lay before them an abstract of the discourse delivered by the first of these gentlemen at opening of his course lectures on natural philosophy, as published in the Journal de Paris . . . as relates to his aerial voyage." Collins reprinted J. A. C. Charles's own description of his ascension, the second in the history of aerial flight, near Paris.

There was room in the paper for less ponderous commentary. Readers of the Trenton column for August 28, 1786, no doubt mused over this item:

> A correspondent, who is a friend of the fair sex, observes, that the malignant and thoughtless make a practice of stigmatizing female weakness. We are told that the ladies dress their heads extravagantly large, but do not the men do the same?—It is said, and with an air of triumph too, that ladies use *lotions* to make their skins fair, and do

not the men do the same?—In short, ransack every female imperfection, display them to view, exaggerate their extravagance—and then dispassionately examine their imperfections of men, and you will find them no less absurd.

Subscribers probably breathed easier after reading the following report in the paper for August 8, 1781: "At a special court lately held in Burlington, a certain Joseph Mulliner of Egg-Harbour, was convicted of high treason and is sentenced to be hanged this day. This fellow had become the terror of that part of the country. He had made a practice of burning houses, robbing and plundering ALL who fell in his way, so that when he came to trial it appeared that the whole country, both Whigs and Tories, were his enemies." Mulliner, a legend in his time, was seen by some as a roguish Robin Hood, by others as a treacherous, crafty scoundrel. He was of that breed known as "Refugees," supposedly loyal to the King, who ravaged the countryside and terrorized housewives while their men were off at war.[12]

An interesting feature of eighteenth-century newspapers was the death notice. Unlike today's factual accounts, the early obituaries were emotional and sentimental, perhaps owing to the strong belief in a life after death. In the *Gazette* for March 19, 1783, Collins noted the passing of a prominent New Jerseyan in this fashion:

New-Brunswick, March 12, 1783

On Tuesday the 4th instant departed this life, James Neilson, Esq. in the 83d year of his age. He had been an extensive trader for many years in this part of the country, and was universally esteemed for his candour and integrity in that profession—Just and upright in all his dealings to such a degree, that envy itself never had an opportunity to detract from his merit—Few men in publick employment have supported so unblemished a character for such a length of time as he did. —Though far advanced in life at the commencement of this unhappy war, his idea of the injustice aimed at his country was clear and unveiled—*He* was exceeded by no character in patriotism.

A major portion of the *Gazette*'s news columns naturally was given over to the more or less official government pronouncements such as proclamations from the governor, legislative acts and resolutions, notices to the militia, depreciation lists and laws specifically designed to control prices. To conserve paper Collins was accustomed to printing the Votes and Proceedings of the Assembly in consecutive issues of the paper rather than separately in pamphlet form. In addition, Collins gave special attention to acts which were relevant to the war effort, that is, the prohibition on exporting provisions from the state and the prevention of New Jersey subjects from going into, or coming out of, enemy lines without permission or passports. In October 1778 he published New Jersey's state constitution, adopted two years before, and in two consecutive numbers of the *Gazette* for January and February 1779 he printed the "Treaty of Amity and Commerce" between France and America. The first official recognition of the United States of America by France, it had been signed on February 6, 1778, by Conrad-Alexandre Gérard, the first French minister to the United States, and Benjamin Franklin, Silas Deane, and Arthur Lee for the new nation.

On August 29 and September 5, 1781, Collins reported on the June 23 military engagement at Springfield, the battle which ended more than five years of active warfare in New Jersey. News circulated quickly on Cornwallis' surrender at Yorktown on October 19, but it took Collins six months to acquire a full report for publication in the *Gazette*. Although this put an end to British offensive efforts in North America, the diplomats took another year to agree at the conference table. The preliminary articles of the peace treaty were signed in Paris on November 30, 1782, but not until the following September did they appear in the *Gazette*. The editor did publish in the meantime—on April 16—Governor Livingston's proclamation declaring the war ended. Collins also reported the signing of the definitive Treaty of Paris, which took place on September 3, 1783, and ratification by the United States on January 14, 1784. The delay was unreasonable, considering the urgencies of peace, for as historian Richard B. Morris believes: "The debates in Congress over ratification and the irresponsbility of many of its delegates constitute one of the less creditable episodes in the history of the central agency of the Confederation whose prestige had declined almost to the vanishing point." [13] In a letter to John Jay, one of the American negotiators and the son-in-law of Governor Livingston, Charles Thomson, Congress' secretary, remarked: "There has been a scene for six months past over which I would wish to draw a veil." [14]

Collins managed to clip from other newspapers "human interest" aspects of the arduous treaty negotiations in France. From London came this story, as it appeared in the *Gazette* for April 30, 1783:

> When Dr. Franklin was about to sign the provisional
> treaty with Mr. Fitzherbert [Alleyne Fitzherbert, a mem-
> ber of the British delegation], at Paris, he begged to leave
> them for a few minutes, which he did, and returned soon
> after in an old suit of clothes, instead of a rich suit in
> which he had just appeared. Being asked the reason of this
> extraordinary circumstance, the veteran answered—"It
> was in this suit that ———— abused me before the privy
> council, and in this suit I chuse to sign the treaty of Ameri-
> can independence."

Such defiance on the part of a distinguished American
patriot, even though false, was the kind of information
patriots back home would have delighted in reading. It is
true that Franklin had been abused in 1774 for his role in
revealing the confidential letters of Massachusetts' Tory
Governor Thomas Hutchison. He was dismissed from
his post as deputy postmaster general for America. Now,
on the occasion of his triumph, he was alleged to have
changed into the suit he had worn on that humiliating
occasion. However, Morris, whose *The Peacemakers* is
the definitive study of the Paris negotiations, dispenses
with the story by saying that "the doctor never left the
room, never changed his coat, and wore at the signing
ceremony a suit of black cloth in keeping with the period
of mourning which had been decreed by the court of
Versailles for the demise of a German prince. When the
story was later called to his attention he indignantly dis-
claimed it." [15] Collins could not have been aware of the
story's inaccuracy, for it circulated widely at the time as
a true account.

Even before the end of the war public attention had
been turning more and more to nonmilitary and non-

political affairs. Collins published extensive news on such topics as education, agriculture, medicine, and finance, reflecting the new interests of the public. Special events at the Trenton area grammar schools and the Trenton Academy, which Collins helped to establish, and at Queen's College (now Rutgers) and at the College of New Jersey were faithfully reported. Schoolmasters gleaned from the *Gazette* advice on the preparation required for admission to the College of New Jersey, whose president, Rev. John Witherspoon, urged the tutors to teach the rules of syntax, to build extensive vocabularies in their pupils, to teach boys to read and pronounce properly, and, "of first importance," accuracy in knowledge of their mother tongue. Collins devoted space on the first page of the March 1, 1780, issue to an act passed in Pennsylvania for the "gradual" abolition of slavery. He reported developments within the New-Jersey Society for Promoting Agriculture, Commerce and Arts, and announced meetings of the state medical society and the Trenton Library Company. On June 6, 1781, the first page of the *Gazette* carried a plan for establishing a national bank, as presented and approved by Congress. Subscribers also learned about adult self-improvement classes in such subjects as singing and the French language.

While the nation rejoiced in having won independence, Collins still faced an old problem as a newspaper editor. His last major engagement in behalf of freedom of the press arose over efforts to suppress the *Gazette* in the spring of 1784. In February the editor had acknowledged receipt of several essays from Governor Livingston, his first batch since the legislative attack on the "Hortentius" articles. Collins, mindful of the earlier "Cincinnatus" affairs, wrote Livingston for instructions. "If any Thing should be thought actionable by the Person referred to in the first," he said, "I suppose it is always understood, that the author, and not the Printer, is to bear the Expenses of such Prosecution; but the author's Name shall be kept a profound Secret, unless ordered to be communicated." [16]

On February 24 one of Livingston's first essays as "Scipio" appeared in the *Gazette*. The butt of the article was Samuel Tucker, who eight years before had been charged with accepting British protection. More damning was the charge that Tucker, as a government official, had misplaced, lost, or stolen public funds. "Scipio" accused the Council of failing to enlist the support of the Assembly for a complete investigation into Tucker's conduct before acquitting him. Although there was some real doubt about Tucker's devotion to the patriot cause, there was also his opposition to Livingston's reelection in 1783 and the next year. Tucker's had been the only dissident voice among the legislators in 1783 and one of four in 1784, which was no doubt an additional grievance to the governor.

Tucker's answer to "Scipio" appeared in the March 2 edition. "Come forth Scipio," he wrote, "give up your name, and I will dissect your performance, and hold you up to the publick in your true colors." Next, Tucker called on Collins at the printing office and tried to get him to reveal the author's name. The editor refused. Tucker, a determined Trenton merchant who had been president of the Provincial Congress in 1776, did succeed in bringing some community pressure to bear on Collins. He claimed that "no anonymous Author has a legal right to attack any Man's publick or private Character without leaving his Name with the Printer," and, as Collins reported to Livingston, Tucker's view "is swallowed pretty generally here by his Advocates." Furthermore, he told the governor: "The People at large want Information on this hand, and I must beg the Favor of you to explain the Matter." [17] What followed represented the combined work of Collins and Livingston to defend, conclusively they hoped, the liberty of the press. [18]

The central issue discussed in "Scipio's" five-part series was the matter of truth as a defense against libel. "All that a writer . . . is to look to, is, that his accusations be true; or at least so probably founded, that he cannot be supposed to be instigated by malevolence." This of course echoes the celebrated Zenger case of 1735, in which Andrew Hamilton, coached by James Alexander, insisted: "*Truth* ought to govern the whole Affair of Libels." [19] Such was thought to be the battle cry of eighteenth-century libertarians, but even after the war, as state constitutions were being framed, nine of them guaranteeing freedom of the press, the old English common law on seditious libel still prevailed. "Scipio's" view is explicit in the following passage:

> Printers often innocently publish what is false, believing it to be true. —Were they to be liable for such error, I know not what news they could give us, without first applying to the court of chancery for a commission to examine witnesses in foreign parts, to ascertain the facts they find already published in the gazettes from which they select their intelligence.
>
> Suppose, for instance, that a Printer in New-Jersey, meeting with the following article in a Maryland Gazette, "That Patrick M'Murrough had been there executed for

a burglary," should re-print it in his newspaper, believing it to be true; Mr. M'Murrough being all the while in full life, and never having committed any burglary—would an action of slander lie for this against the Jersey Printer? I think not. And hence it is that in the English law, notwithstanding its ineffable nonsense of making the printing of truth more atrocious than the printing of lies, still charges every libel in the process against the author of it to be not only *false,* but *malicious,* clearly affording the most violent implication that even a falsity unattended with *malice* (and such ought to be presumed every falsity which the publisher believed to be true) is not culpable. By this it also appears how flatly they contradict their own doctrine, that falsehood is more innocent than truth. . . .[20]

Livingston's position in the "Scipio" essays was strongly libertarian, but state legislatures, in acting on the proposed Bill of Rights several years later, apparently had little serious understanding of "liberty of the press." In fact, as Leonard W. Levy shows, "the history of the ratification indicates no passion on the part of anyone to grind underfoot the common law. . . ." [21] Collins himself advocated freedom of expression short of seditious libel. He believed that a person might say anything on condition he did so with a regard for the laws. In a sense, his view was similar to that of Benjamin Franklin in that a publisher should regard himself as a "Guardian of his Country's Reputation, and refuse to insert such Writings as may hurt it." [22] The American states, Levy asserts, did not take the opportunity of abandoning or seriously limiting the oppressive common law of seditious libel.[23] New Jersey, unlike its neighbor Pennsylvania, did not even provide for freedom of speech in its constitution.

Collins, nevertheless, helped promote the idea that truth was a defense against libel. His courteous yet firm refusal to yield to outside pressure, including that of the legislature, represents an early stand for the liberty of the press. Collins's position appears strong in light of the fact that no one possessed a legal right to free speech until the nation's First Amendment was ratified in 1791, nearly ten years after the end of a war fought to get rid of the British law.

The end of the year 1786 brought the demise of the *New-Jersey Gazette*. The edition for November 27 carried this notice, conspicuous for its brevity: "This day's Gazette, No. 446, completes the year. The little encouragement given to the circulation of it during the last eighteen months, and the impossibility of collecting payment, have determined the Printer to drop the publication. In every other respect the Printing Business will be carried on as usual, and performed in a correct, neat and expeditious manner." The end came suddenly, but not unexpectedly. When the *Gazette* was established nine years before, Collins had promised to print legislative news, useful and entertaining essays, "schemes" for the advancement of trade, arts, and manufacturing, and ideas for improving agriculture, in short, "a faithful Account of remarkable Occurrences whether foreign or domestic." As publisher and editor of what started out as a state-subsidized newspaper, he was perhaps under a greater obligation to serve the public interest, which was at that time the patriot cause, than were other early American printers. Long after his obligation to the state ceased, Collins continued to edit a newspaper remarkable for its balanced treatment of colonial and early state affairs.

Like Benjamin Franklin, who used to call his newspaper debts "an Estate in the Clouds," Isaac Collins returned full time to his other printing enterprises, which were to provide the foundation for his subsequent financial success.[24]

By the time the *New-Jersey Gazette* ceased publication two other newspapers had been started in the state. In May 1786 Shepard Kollock had resumed publication of his *New-Jersey Journal* in Elizabethtown. This paper had been started in 1779 in Chatham and ended in 1783, when Kollock moved first to New Brunswick and then to Elizabethtown to publish another paper, the *Political Intelligencer, and New-Jersey Advertiser*. Still published today, the *Journal* is New Jersey's oldest newspaper and the fourth oldest in the country. On October 5, 1786, about a month before Collins ended the *Gazette,* the state's third regular newspaper was founded by Shelly Arnett, Kollock's brother-in-law and former associate in New Brunswick. It was called the *New-Brunswick Gazette, and Weekly Monitor,* and today, the nation's fifth oldest continuously published paper, it is known as the *Daily Home News*.[25]

The year 1786 in New Jersey, though a fateful one for Collins's paper, bears out the observation of an early historian "that the eighteenth century may be emphatically called *the age of periodical publications*." [26] In that year James Tod established the *Princeton Packet and General Advertiser,* the state's fourth regular newspaper, which signaled the first attempt to fill the void left by the *Gazette* in the Trenton area. Although it ceased publication after a year, it was later revived and is still published as a weekly in Princeton. On May 15, 1787, less than a year after Collins stopped the *Gazette,* Frederick Quequelle and George M. Wilson started the *Trenton Mercury and Weekly Advertiser.* It lasted only until January 1789, but it was the first semiweekly newspaper in New Jersey.

Quequelle had previously started a magazine in New Brunswick with James Prange, hoping to compete with Arnett's newspaper. It was called the *New-Jersey Magazine, and Monthly Advertiser,* the first in the state since James Parker's *New American Magazine,* published in 1758–60. But the magazine lasted for only three months during 1786–87, the victim of competition, whereupon Quequelle moved to Trenton and Prange to Philadelphia to publish the *Evening Chronicle.*

New Jerseyans in the closing years of the century witnessed the birth of other newspapers in the state. The first paper in Newark, for instance, was started on May 19, 1791, by John Woods, a former apprentice to Kollock. He called it *Woods' Newark Gazette.* On September 12, 1792, two years after Trenton became the state capital, the *New-Jersey State Gazette* was launched by Mathias Day in silent partnership with George F. Hopkins. They changed the name in 1796 to the *State Gazette, and New-Jersey Advertiser* and three years later sold it to George Sherman and John Mershon, who restored the original title. Daniel Dodge and Aaron Pennington of Newark introduced the *Centinel of Freedom* on October 5, 1796, the year after Philip Freneau had started the *Jersey Chronicle* at his ancestral home at Mount Pleasant (now Matawan) in Monmouth County.[27]

During this brief period three more magazines appeared on the scene. In April 1794 John Woods started the *United States Magazine;* in the summer and fall of 1797 Daniel Dodge printed *A Magazine* for Moses N. Combs; and in February 1798 John H. Williams began publishing the *Rural Magazine.* All were issued from printing shops in Newark, which had become the state's printing center.

Between December 1777, when Collins first issued the *New-Jersey Gazette,* and 1800, more than twenty newspapers, not to mention a few magazines, were begun in New Jersey. Most of them were failures; but at the turn of the century New Jersey had six newspapers: the *Newark Gazette;* the *Centinel of Freedom,* also of Newark; the *New-Jersey State Gazette* in Trenton; the *Genius of Liberty* in Morristown; the *Guardian, or New-Brunswick Advertiser;* and the *New-Jersey Journal* in Elizabeth.

Isaac Collins in 1806, two years before his retirement. Oil by
John Wesley Jarvis. (Courtesy of Grellet N. Collins, Chestertown, Maryland. Photograph by Constance Stuart Larrabee.)

THE

HISTORY

OF THE CHRISTIAN PEOPLE CALLED

QUAKERS.

THE FIRST BOOK.

THAT the wonderful WORK of Reformation was fmall, and of very little account in its beginning, and yet hath been advanced with remarkable progrefs, will, I believe, be denied by none, that have with attention and due confideration read the hiftory of its firft rife; fince God, the beginner and author of this glorious work, proceeding by fteps and degrees, ufed therein fuch fingular wifdom and prudence, that every circumftance duly confidered, inftead of cenfuring any part thereof, we fhall be obliged to cry out, Thou, O Lord, alone know'ft the right times and feafons to open the eyes of people, and to make them capable of thy Truth!

If we look to the firft beginnings, to go back no farther than John Hus, we fhall find, that though in many things he was conſiderably enlightened, yet he remained ftill in feveral grofs errors; for altho' he had a clear fight of the vain doctrines of purgatory, praying to, and worfhipping of images, &c. neverthelefs it is reported of him, that he favoured the invocation of faints, the feven facraments, auricular confeffion, and other tenets of the church of Rome; and yet chriftian charity conftrains us to believe (tho' we find proteftant writers who deny him the name of a martyr) that by his death, which he fuffered in the flames at Conftance in Germany, on the fixth of the month called July, in the year 1415, he was an acceptable facrifice unto God: and with what a fedate and well compofed mind he fuffered death, may be concluded from this, that feeing a country fellow very zealoufly carrying wood to burn him, he faid, with a fmiling countenance, 'O holy fimplicity!' And after the fire was kindled, he fang with joy in the flames, his mind being firmly eftablifhed on God; for he had been faithful according to his knowledge, and had not hid his talent in the earth, but improved it, having fhewn himfelf a zealous promoter of that fmall illumination which God was pleafed to grant him;

D   it

1415.

J. Hus, an early reformer, burnt for Religion.

The opening of the first book of William Sewel's *History of the Rise, Increase and Progress of the Christian People Called Quakers*, printed by Isaac Collins in Burlington in 1774. (Courtesy of the Rutgers University Library.)

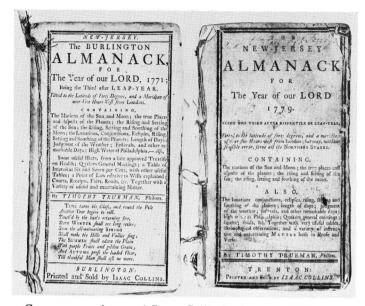

Cover pages of two of Isaac Collins's almanacs. (Courtesy
of the Rutgers University Library.) *Below:* The Burling-
ton Friends' Meeting on North High Street, built in 1784.
Scene drawn on stone by John Collins, grandson of Isaac
Collins and a watercolor artist and lithographer, active
1833-1869. Printed by Thomas Sinclair of Philadelphia.
(From John Collins, *Views of the City of Burlington, New
Jersey,* Burlington, 1847.)

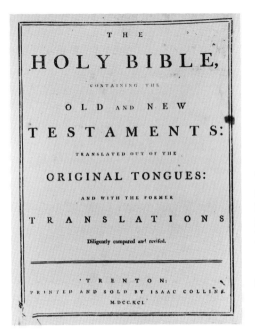

Title pages of the second quarto edition of the King James Bible to be printed in America, 1791; Job Scott's *Journal,* 1797; and David Ramsay's *History of the Revolution of South-Carolina,* 1785. (Courtesy of the Rutgers University Library.)

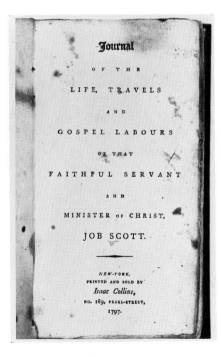

Journal

OF THE

LIFE, TRAVELS

AND

GOSPEL LABOURS

OF THAT

FAITHFUL SERVANT

AND

MINISTER OF CHRIST,

JOB SCOTT.

NEW-YORK,

PRINTED AND SOLD BY

Isaac Collins,

NO. 189, PEARL-STREET,

1797.

THE

HISTORY

OF THE

REVOLUTION

OF

SOUTH-CAROLINA,

FROM A BRITISH PROVINCE

TO AN INDEPENDENT STATE.

BY DAVID RAMSAY, M. D.

MEMBER OF THE AMERICAN CONGRESS.

IN TWO VOLUMES.

VOL. I.

TRENTON:

PRINTED BY ISAAC COLLINS.

M.DCC.LXXXV.

Isaac Collins's printing office in Burlington, New Jersey, from 1770 to 1778. Watercolor by Collins's grandson John Collins in 1889. (Courtesy of George C. Rockefeller, Madison, New Jersey.) *Below:* Paper currency emitted by the Colony of New Jersey on March 25, 1776. Printed by Isaac Collins, printer to the King. (Courtesy of the Rutgers University Library.)

[VOL. I.]

T H E

NEW-JERSEY GAZETTE.

[NUMB. 22.]

WEDNESDAY, APRIL 29, 1778.

The following is published by order of the General Assembly of this State, for the confideration of the inhabitants thereof.

ARTICLES of CONFEDERATION and perpetual UNION between the States of New-Hampfhire, Maffachufetts-Bay, Rhode-Ifland and Providence Plantations, Connecticut, New-York, New-Jerfey, Pennfylvania, Delaware, Maryland, Virginia, North-Carolina, South-Carolina and Georgia.

A R T I C L E I.

THE ftile of this confederacy fhall be "The United States of America."

Art. II. Each State retains its fovereignty, freedom and independence, and every power, jurifdiction and right, which is not by this confederation exprefly delegated to the United States in Congrefs affembled.

Art. III. The faid States hereby feverally enter into a firm league of friendfhip with each other, for their common defence, the fecurity of their liberties, and their mutual and general welfare, binding themfelves to affift each other, againft all force offered to them, or attacks made upon them, or any of them, on account of religion, fovereignty, trade, or any other pretence whatever.

Art. IV. The better to fecure and perpetuate mu-

without the confent of the United States in Congrefs affembled, fpecifying accurately the purpose for which the fame is to be entered into, and how long it fhall continue.

No State fhall lay any impofts or duties, which may interfere with any ftipulations in treaties entered into by the United States in Congrefs affembled, with any King, Prince or State, in purfuance of any treaties already propofed by Congrefs, to the courts of France and Spain.

No veffels of war fhall be kept up in time of peace by any State, except fuch number only, as fhall be deemed neceffary by the United States in Congrefs affembled, for the defence of fuch State or its trade; nor fhall any body of forces be kept up by any State, in time of peace, except fuch number only, as in the judgement of the United States in Congrefs affembled, fhall be deemed requifite to garrifon the forts neceffary for the defence of fuch State; but every State fhall always keep up a well regulated and difciplined militia, fufficiently armed and accoutred, and fhall provide and conftantly have ready for ufe, in public ftores, a due number of field pieces and tents, and a proper quantity of arms, ammunition and camp equipage.

No State fhall engage in any war without the confent of the United States in Congrefs affembled, unlefs fuch State be actually invaded by enemies, or

thority, or lawful agent of any State in controverfy with another fhall prefent a petition to Congrefs ftating the matter in queftion and praying for a hearing, notice thereof fhall be given by order of Congrefs to the legiflative or executive authority of the other State in controverfy, and a day affigned for the appearance of the parties by their lawful agents, who fhall then be directed to appoint by joint confent, commiffioners or judges to conftitute a court for hearing and determining the matter in queftion; but if they cannot agree, Congrefs fhall name three perfons out of each of the United States, and from the lift of fuch perfons each party fhall alternately ftrike out one, the petitioners beginning, until the number fhall be reduced to thirteen; and from that number not lefs than feven, nor more than nine names, as Congrefs fhall direct, fhall in the prefence of Congrefs be drawn out by lot, and the perfons whofe names fhall be drawn or any five of them, fhall be commiffioners or judges, to hear and finally determine the controverfy, fo always as a major part of the judges who fhall hear the caufe fhall agree in the determination; and if either party fhall neglect to attend at the day appointed, without fhewing reafons, which Congrefs fhall judge fufficient, or being prefent fhall refufe to ftrike, the Congrefs fhall proceed to nominate three perfons out of each State, and the Secretary of Congrefs fhall ftrike in behalf of fuch

State of New-Jersey

1796.
6 mo: 27, To printing 1000 Copies of the Votes,
and Proceedings of the Assembly of
New-Jersey, 2d Sitting 20th Session
containing 16½ Sheets, 8 d'y ⅌ Sheet £ 66:0:0

To Isaac Collins Dr

Received July 4th 1796 of James Mott treas'r Sixty six —
Pounds in full of the Above Account
£ 66 . 0 . 0

Isaac Collins.

Isaac Collins's receipted bill to the state of New Jersey for printing 1,000 copies of the Votes and Proceedings of the General Assembly's twentieth session, second sitting, 1796. (Courtesy of the Trenton Free Public Library.)

A C T S

OF THE

General Affembly

OF THE PROVINCE OF

NEW-JERSEY,

FROM THE

Surrender of the Government to Queen ANNE, on the 17th Day of *April*,
in the Year of our Lord 1702, to the 14th Day of *January* 1776.

TO WHICH IS ANNEXED.

The ORDINANCE for regulating and eftablifhing the FEES
of the COURT of CHANCERY of the faid Province.

WITH THREE ALPHABETICAL TABLES, AND AN INDEX.

Compiled and publifhed under the Appointment of the GENERAL ASSEMBLY, and
compared with the ORIGINAL ACTS,

By SAMUEL ALLINSON.

MUNICIPAL LAW is a Rule of civil Conduct prefcribed by the Supreme Power in a State, commanding what is
RIGHT and prohibiting what is WRONG. 1 *Black. Com.* 44.
The REASON of the Law is the Life of the Law. 2 *Ab. Ca.* Eq. 400.
No Freeman fhall be taken or imprifoned, or be diffeifed of his Freehold, or Liberties or free Cuftoms, or be out-
lawed, or exiled, or any otherwise deftroyed, nor we will not pafs upon him, nor condemn him, but by LAWFUL
JUDGMENT of his Peers or by LAW OF THE LAND. We will SELL to no Man, we will not DENY or DEFER
to any Man either JUSTICE or RIGHT. *Magna Charta*, Chap. XXXIX.

BURLINGTON:

Printed by ISAAC COLLINS, Printer to the King, for the Province of *New-Jerfey*.
M.DCC.LXXVI.

Title page of Samuel Allinson's compilation of the Acts of the New Jersey General Assembly, April 17, 1702, to January 14, 1776, printed for the Province in 1776 by Isaac Collins. (Courtesy of the Rutgers University Library.)

Wooden press and type case from the printing house of Isaiah Thomas of Worcester, Massachusetts. The "old-fashioned" English press remained in common use in England and America through most of the eighteenth century, even though some printers considered its mechanism inferior to that of Dutch models. (Courtesy of the Museum of the American Antiquarian Society, Worcester, Mass.)

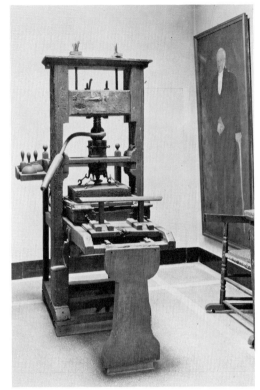

❦ V ❧

MERCHANT
AND CITIZEN

Quaker merchants of the eighteenth century, Frederick B. Tolles reminds us, possessed a "single-minded devotion to mercantile pursuits and exceptional business acumen." [1] Isaac Collins—printer, publisher, bookseller, merchant—was of this tradition. Trenton, when Collins moved there in 1778, promised to become the main city between New York and Philadelphia. It was a bustling city of commercial and, to a lesser degree, cultural activity. Travelers through the Middle States seeking business or pleasure usually paused there and by so doing helped to spread knowledge of the town both in this country and abroad. Collins's printing office on the southeast corner of State and Broad Streets, the center of town, was a popular meeting place for sojourners. So many Friends, for instance, made his shop and home their temporary headquarters that the Collins establishment came to be known as the "Quaker Tavern." [2]

During the time the Collins printing house published the weekly *New-Jersey Gazette,* the master printer's career flourished, with respect both to his other printing and publishing enterprises and to his involvement in Trenton civic affairs. In 1779 Collins issued a second book by the Quaker writer Anthony Benezet, entitled *The Mighty Destroyer Displayed.* A small volume, in the author's words it dealt with "the havock made by the mistaken use as well as abuse of distilled spirituous liquors." The next significant imprint to come from Collins's press was an edition in 1780 of the *New England Primer,* perhaps the most popular of all early American textbooks. It contained many typically Puritan verses written to expose children to the fear of death, thus purging them of original sin. This prayer, still recited today, appeared in the *Primer:*

> If I should die before I wake
> I pray the Lord my soul to take.

More frightening were these lines:

> I in the burying-place may see
>   Graves shorter there than I;
> From Death's arrest no age is free;
>   Young children, too, may die.
>
> My God, may such an awful sight
>   Awakening be to me!
> O that by early grace I might
>   For death prepared to be!

Of wide appeal also was a funeral sermon delivered by Samuel Stanhope Smith, president of the College of New Jersey, on the death of Richard Stockton in 1781. Stockton, an eminent lawyer and former member of the royal governor's Council, was the most prominent New Jersey signer of the Declaration of Independence. His home was Morven in Princeton, now the official residence of the state's governor.

In the days toward the end of the war, a war that had precipitated a general laxity in moral and religious training, Collins was among a handful of Trenton citizens who set out to reaffirm the importance of education to community progress. On the evening of February 10, 1781, Collins and about twenty other townsmen met for the express purpose of founding the Trenton School Company. They were in step with their contemporaries, for in that year also Queen's College reopened in New Brunswick after its precarious existence during hostilities in New Jersey. The state medical society was also revived in 1781, and New Jersey had begun a new era of cultural growth. The Trenton School Company was a major factor in this renascence.

Collins was elected to the five-member board of trustees of the School Company. As the owner of the town's printing house and, more important, the publisher and editor of the newspaper, he was a prominent citizen. The other board members, all of whom Collins knew either in business or politics, were Stacy Potts, Moore Furman, James Ewing, and William Churchill Houston. Potts, one of Trenton's leading industrialists, had at various times operated a steel factory, a tannery, and a paper mill. He was elected clerk.

Furman, then a judge, had served New Jersey as deputy quartermaster general during most of the war, and, in this critical post, bought writing paper, ink, and quills from Collins for military correspondence. Collins probably knew Ewing best; their friendship eventually grew into a brief business partnership. Ewing later became mayor of Trenton. Houston, an educational and political force in New Jersey's early history, had been a friend of the printer for several years, noticeably since the inception of the *Gazette,* which Houston as a member of the state legislature helped establish.[3]

Originally, the school company's stock consisted of $750 divided into thirty-six shares. Possession of a share gave the owner the right to send a child to the Trenton Academy, an undenominational school, without charge for use of the building. In other words, students whose parents did not own shares were assessed a rental fee in addition to the tuition everyone paid. Collins, the father of six at the time of the Academy's formation, not only subscribed liberally over the years, but eventually paid for the tuition of nine of his fourteen children.

First, however, the Academy had to be built. By May 1781 the trustees had raised enough money to buy the land, a sizable lot on Fourth Street (now Hanover) owned by Moore Furman. Early the next year the students and their instructor, James Burnside, moved into the two-room structure. Collins and Rensselaer Williams, a farmer and justice of the peace, were appointed "visitors" to observe Burnside's teaching methods. They said they found him "attentive to his duty, the School in decent order and an uncommon degree of emulation for improvement seems to prevail among the scholars." [4] They also reported to the trustees that "good attention is paid to spelling, reading, and writing, and Jacob Benjamin, Charles Highbee, William Pearson, Wilson Hunt, John Clunn, John Trenton, Hill Runyon, John Hunt, Rensselaer Williams, Noah Davis, Samuel Dickenson, Rebecca Collins, Elizabeth Williams, and Elizabeth Crolins are learning arithmetick." On a later inspection Collins and Williams found proper decorum kept by the master and improvement in the scholars.

From the printing house in 1782 came an edition of another perennial favorite in the Middle States, *Philosophic Solitude, or The Choice of a Rural Life,* the long pastoral poem by Governor Livingston. Not only was the poem very popular after it was first published in 1747; it is often cited by literary historians as Livingston's best poetic effort. Charles Angoff asserts that he was the principal poet in New York before the Revolution. Livingston belonged to a circle of writers that included Mather Byles, William Smith, and the Connecticut poets John Trumbull, Timothy Dwight, and Joel Barlow, all of whom wrote chiefly for the erudite and the sophisticated wealthy.[5] Written when Livingston was only twenty-four years old, it describes pleasant pastimes to be enjoyed in the quiet of rural life, pronouncing them preferable to the bustle of the city:

> Let ardent heroes seek renown in arms,
> Pant after fame, and rush to war's alarms;
> To shining palaces, let fools resort,
> And dunces cringe to be esteemed at court;

Mine be the pleasures of rural life,
From noise remote, and ignorant of strife;
Far from the painted belle, the white-gloved beau,
The lawless masquerade and midnight show;
From ladies, lap dogs, courtiers, garters, stars,
Fops, fiddlers, tyrants, Emperors, and Czars.

The poem's appeal no doubt lay in Livingston's ability to reflect the suppressed desires of people living in a materially oriented city. In reissuing *Philosophic Solitude,* however, Collins was more likely motivated by its sales potential as an early work by New Jersey's governor. The poem eventually went through at least five printings.

There is no reason to believe that Livingston's major poem was required reading at the Trenton Academy, although the students did study contemporary works as well as the classics. But these were limited to works on writing, arithmetic, geography, and the "English Language grammatically." They read "what is usually read in Schools" of Caesar's *Commentaries,* Ovid's *Metamorphoses,* and Justin or Sallust in Latin, and could select any two of the following: the New Testament, Lucian's *Dialogues,* or Xenophon or Homer in Greek. As a reward for this extra effort, the students were entitled to have their classical subjects inscribed on their diplomas. Optional subjects, such as the modern foreign languages, were available to advanced students. Collins's daughter Rebecca was permitted to study French, knowledge of which in later life became more than purely academic to her as the wife of Stephen Grellet (Etienne de Grellet du Mabillier). Charles and Thomas Collins graduated with honors from the Academy. Another daughter, Ann, was judged the third best reader in her class in 1796, for which she received as her "Reward of Merit" an inscribed copy of the *Lady's Pocket Library*.[6]

Collins, as a trustee, affixed his signature to most of the Academy's important documents, including the diplomas presented "to such scholars as shall have studied the English language grammatically." In addition to literature, the students were expected to have gained a "competent knowledge" of at least two of the following disciplines: Extraction of the Roots, Algebra, Mathematics, Geography, Chronology, History, Logic, Rhetoric, Moral and Natural Philosophy, and the Spirit of Laws and Criticism. Collins remained active on the board of trustees for all but a couple of years during his residence in Trenton, or until his move to New York in 1796.[7]

When the proprietors of the Trenton School Company, as owners of the Trenton Academy, started their educational project they were helping to give impetus to one of the most significant periods in the history of New Jersey education. The establishment of the academy in American educational life provided a transition from the classical tradition of the old grammar school to the democratic and pragmatic concept of the high school. The academy, says one historian, "perfectly fitted a period of cultural transition, blending the classical and the modern spirits in the community sense of a growing young republic." [8]

Trenton was not the only New Jersey community with such an institution. Between 1780 and 1795 schools of "useful knowledge" were located in Newark, Elizabethtown, Hackensack, Morristown, Orange Dale (now Orange), Middletown, Woodbury, and Salem—in short, all over the state. The new emphasis on practical studies, spurred by the general spirit of nationalism after the war, may be seen in the Trenton curriculum. Besides the specific subjects already noted, Democracy, Equality, and Utility became terms in education as they did in other areas of national interest. The academies "admitted children of the common people, opened their doors to girls, and stressed preparation for ordinary life." [9]

In 1783, a year after the Trenton School Company opened its two-room Academy, the increase in the number of proprietors, or shareholders, and the subsequent growth of its endowment enabled the construction of two more rooms. In 1785 the trustees successfully petitioned the state legislature to pass an act incorporating the original proprietors and trustees. The Trenton Academy had become a permanent part of the community and the state.

Because early American printing houses, particularly those that published newspapers, were places of congregation for townspeople, it was smart business practice for Collins to add notions, stationery, and groceries, a variety of merchandise, to his shop. He frequently advertised in the *Gazette* as follows: "A quantity of capital MEDICINES, viz. Epsom's Salts, Jesuit's Bark, Gum Manna, Glister Pipes [and] a few chests of TEA warranted the first quality for Bohea." In January 1782 he offered for sale "on the lowest terms of cash only" coffee, tea, spices, needles, and pottery. By June he had stocked, in his words, "Excellent West India and country Rum and Whiskey."

This part of the business prospered, but the staple items of the press still brought the major part of the firm's income. In 1782 and 1783 respectively Collins reprinted works by Thomas Paine and Anthony Benezet, the latter's a volume in the continuing antislavery movement among Quakers. The decade of the 1780's, if not Collins's busiest as a printer, was certainly his most important as a merchant and a citizen.

Sometime during 1783 Collins entered into a merchandising partnership with his old friend James Ewing, who at one time had been New Jersey state auditor and later became mayor of Trenton. They first operated their store at the printing office but soon moved to larger quarters, announced in the *Gazette* for July 2: "Collins and Ewing—Have removed their store to the house in which Mr. James Paxton lately lived, directly opposite Samuel Tucker's Esq., in Trenton, where they have just opened a very general assortment of European, East and West India goods, suitable for the season, which they are selling on the lowest terms for cash or country produce."

The partnership, separate from Collins's printing business, lasted only three years. Issues of the *Gazette* for 1786, the final year of its publication, contain front-page notices of the dissolution. One cannot help but wonder about the friendship that may, or may not, have existed between Collins and his neighbor Tucker before, as well as after, the heated "Scipio" affair during the spring of 1784.

In discussing eighteenth-century commerce, one must inevitably enter into the debate over the distinction between the terms "merchant" and "shopkeeper." Johnson's *Dictionary* defines the merchant as "one who trafficks to remote countries," which Collins did not do, although much of the merchandise he sold was imported from abroad and purchased in this country through shipping companies. Dr. Johnson's definition of the shopkeeper is the same as his definition of a tradesman, but with this distinction: "A merchant is called a *trader*, but not a tradesman; and it seems distinguished in Shakespeare from a man that labours with his hands. 'I live by the awl, I meddle with no *tradesmen's* matters.' "

A writer in the *New-Jersey Gazette* for May 24, 1784, distinguishes between merchant and shopkeeper, but he assumes that his readers already know the difference: "The merchant, or rather the shopkeeper (for alas! alas! alas! it is devoutly to be wished that we had a competent number of the first denomination, before we are ground into atoms by Philadelphia and New York). . . ." Since the terms were often disputed and used interchangeably by citizens, it is reasonably correct to say that most of the time Collins was a shopkeeper, or retailer, and at times, when, for example, he sold large quantities of goods to the army, he was a merchant, or wholesaler. At least this was the distinction made by a Hunterdon County, New Jersey, grand jury in 1765.[10]

The distinctions matter only insofar as they help to indicate Collins's social and economic status in Trenton. Although shopkeepers often equaled merchants in riches, they generally were less wealthy and prominent. Some shopkeepers, who were employes rather than independent entrepreneurs, earned from £200 to £500 annually, while others were paid as little as £15 or £25 a year plus "keep." "Probably the average income of the established merchant was well over £500 sterling, while shopkeepers earned less than half of that sum."[11] If Collins earned no more than the average as a merchant-shopkeeper, then his second income as a printer, estimated to have been between £300 and £500, made his total financial worth and social position among the highest in his community.

During as well as after his brief partnership with Ewing, Collins's printing house continued to function also as a general store. He advertised in the *New-Jersey Gazette:* "Testaments, Journals of Congress, Vicar of Wakefield, History of New-Jersey, Allinson's edition of the body of laws of New-Jersey, Dilworth's spelling books, Croxall's Aesop's fables, Horn books, writing paper, powers of attorney, quills, dressed and undressed, black sealing wax, lamp black, Best grey hair powder, Epsom's salts, Bateman's drops, Godfrey's cordial, gum myrrh, camphor."

The New Testaments advertised probably included those issued in 1779 and 1780 from Collins's own presses as well as copies acquired on consignment from other printers. The *Journals of Congress,* which Collins had unsuccessfully bid to publish, were issued by John Dunlap of Philadelphia. They were no doubt a popular commodity in the early years of the new nation. The copies of Oliver Goldsmith's *Vicar of Wakefield* were purchased wholesale from other printers, many perhaps imported from England. Apparently copies of Samuel Smith's *History of the Colony of Nova-Caesaria, or New Jersey,* published by James Parker in 1765, were still available and popular. Samuel Allinson's *Acts* was a major government printing assignment for Collins in 1776. In 1786 he issued Thomas Dilworth's latest text, *A New Guide to the English Tongue.* Robert Aitken, the Philadelphia printer and binder, had been Collins's main source for Croxall's edition of Aesop since 1779.

Quills and writing paper were sold in large quantities to members of the legislature as well as to townspeople.

At one time James Mott, the state treasurer, bought one hundred quills for government use alone. As Trenton's chief stationer, Collins serviced the needs of famous persons, among them Pierre Eugène du Simitière, a French artist and member of the American Philosophical Society.[12]

But, it seems, more than selling merchandise was expected of the shopkeeper. On one occasion that we know of, though there must have been others, Collins prescribed the use of Holme's Poultice Root much in the manner of a druggist: "I . . . inquired of Judge Brearly respecting its Operation—who told me he was not lanced but the Doctor used a Probe—the first or second application is attended with considerable Smarting when the ulcer is lanced but after that it heals remarkably fast and without Pain. We know of several Persons who have used it with great Success." [13]

Yet, even as he divided his time among a number of activities, Collins never got far away from his basic concern for education. After having helped to establish the Trenton Academy, he joined the Trenton Society for Improvement in Useful Knowledge in an effort to broaden his own intellectual horizons. One requirement of membership was the writing of essays to be read, presumably, before the society. Two essays that Collins wrote offer some insight into the personal life and ideas of this industrious and conservative Quaker merchant. Admittedly a stern man in his own family, Collins admired those individuals who, in his words, "feared God and worked righteousness." [14]

One essay, written in 1782, attempts to answer the question: "Whether it would not be for the good of the

Community were the Legislature to repeal so much of the Law 'for preventing clandestine marriages' as enables Persons to marry by License?" He said: "Persons who can produce a Certificate in Writing expressing the Parents or Guardians Consent, and by entering into Bond in the Sum of Five hundred Pounds may marry." He took issue, not with the intent of the marriage-license law, but rather with the fact that it was "eluded and evaded" by the forgery of certificates and the borrowing of the security. The law, Collins opined, was unworkable because it was unrealistic.[15]

He had an alternative proposal. He recommended the abolition of marriage licenses, to be replaced by a form of public announcement. Collins wrote: "I would have the Act in Question amended obliging those who intend to marry, except such as perform this Ceremony agreeably to the Practice of some religious Society, in order to make the Marriage noted, to set up Advertisements notifying their Intention in (say) six of the most publick Places in the Township or Townships where the Parties, so intending to marry reside, one Month before the Marriage takes Place, and also to produce a Certificate as the Law now prescribed from the Parents, Guardians, etc. as the Case may require." If the purpose of the law, in other words, were to prevent secret marriages, then Collins believed it should compel couples to announce their impending marriage publicly. He alluded to the fact that the Quaker sect, among others, already had such a regulation. It was, and is, the custom for Quakers to "declare intentions" at two consecutive monthly meetings, after which permission to marry was officially granted or denied. In effect, then, Collins asked for the enactment of a law endorsing the custom of the Friends and the practice of publishing banns in other denominations.

Collins's second extant essay, written in 1784, also approached its subject rhetorically: "By what means can an Individual in the Capacity of a private Citizen best promote the public Happiness?" Such questions, always of vital importance to citizens, took on even greater significance during the American reconstruction following the Revolution. Peace had come, and men again could devote more attention to philosophical issues.[16]

The essay continued: "In the United States of America, the Asylum for all the Graces of every Country, the greatest Publick Happiness will consist in the Promotion of the greatest private Virtues." Likened in this way to the judgment of God, righteous and just, man's essential happiness "will be readily granted . . . by using Industry, suppressing Vice and promoting Virtue." Collins, here potently Puritan and proud, went on: "Our Ideas of public Happiness may be said to be interwoven in the Mind by the Manner of our Education, or by the Formation of the Government under which we happen to be placed." Thus, in keeping with the spirit of nationalism, the printer argued that happiness could be found in whatever "object" was nearest to the heart of a nation.

In France, we are told that the greatest Glory of the Subject is in implicitly obeying the Royal Decrees of his Sovereign; the Goodwill of his Sovereign there then under the Smiles of Providence, is the Source from whence all publick Happiness flows, and of course he who most distinguishes himself in fulfilling these Requisitions, most promotes the publick Happiness in France.

In the United Netherlands Industry most promotes the

publick Happiness, as it most increases Wealth, the worldly God of that People.

In Britain the Licentiousness of the Press is their greatest Glory, and in which they place their greatest Happiness. This appears in a thousand Instances by their Publications against their King, Lords & Commons and against every other Man in office. In this Business the Gentlemen of the Type are among the foremost, and thereupon in the most delectable Situation.

Collins's severe criticism of his British colleagues was doubtless spurred by his first-hand knowledge of journalistic propaganda during the Revolution, in this country as well as abroad. He declared, however, that "the political Mind of America is yet to form, and in that Proportion we may be considered as capable or incapable of serving Impressions Good or Evil." He continued:

> As I said before, Happiness is no where to be found but in the Mind; it is therefore, thus considered, in our own Option but under the directing Hand of Providence to say to what Degree of Happiness we shall arrive. Happiness was undoubtedly the original Object of all the Nations who have gone before us; and all we have to do is, to mark the Rocks upon which they split, in order to arrive to a greater Degree of it.
>
> Upon the whole it seems *our* national Happiness does not consist in obeying the tyrannical Will of an arbitrary Prince—in the use of a great Quantity of Gold or Silver—in Industry considered only as the Mother of Wealth—nor yet in abusing the Licentiousness of the Press, the administrators of our Government. But it consists in doing all the Good we can for one another, considering at all Times, and almost upon all Occasions, our one great and extensive Family, united by the Ties of Friendship, Interest, and all the Social Virtues.

Perhaps it is a coincidence that the essay on public happiness and the "Scipio" affair occurred in the same year, 1784. Regardless of which side of the Tucker-Livingston debate Collins personally may have defended, it would appear that he sided with the press in most of these controversies. Above all, the highest national authority, the government, was to Collins still the servant of the people, who were united, not by administrators, but by the "Ties of Friendship, Interest, and all the Social Virtues."

Work in the printing shop, meanwhile, was not limited to the weekly *Gazette*. Collins and his employees, numbering among them members of his own family and wandering journeymen, issued government documents, the *New-Jersey Almanack,* and a variety of books, pamphlets, and broadsides. To keep up with the demands on his shop, Collins advertised for printers, pressmen, and apprentices in nearly every issue of the *Gazette,* but especially during the war years when manpower was in short supply. "A good WORKMAN at Press and Case will find constant Business, be exempted from actual Service in the Militia, and receive handsome Wages." Although he depended largely on help from outside his own family, eventually his two oldest sons, Charles and Thomas, joined him. Most of the journeymen who worked for Collins at one time or another came from Philadelphia, where scores of early American printers learned their trade.

Among the printers who joined Collins in Trenton were Samuel Inslee and Anthony Armbruster (Anton Armbrüster). Like many of their kind, both had worked in other colonies.[17] It was Inslee who, in partnership with Anthony Carr, had leased the old James Parker printing house in Woodbridge from Samuel Parker after his father's death in 1770. Inslee and Carr continued the *New-York Gazette; or, the Weekly Post-Boy* for more than two years. Afterwards, however, young Parker, who had lost out to Collins in the contest for government printing in New Jersey, failed to revive his father's publication. Inslee at one time worked for William Goddard in Providence and, presumably, in Philadelphia too. Shortly after Collins moved from Burlington to Trenton in 1778, Inslee joined the business. He died a few years later, reportedly by his own hand.

Armbruster had emigrated from Germany to Philadelphia about 1743 and conducted one of the two entirely German printing houses in Pennsylvania in the 1750's (the other was that of Christopher Sower, Sr.). In 1754 he formed a partnership with Franklin, and the next year they began publication of the *Philadelphische Zeitung.* The paper was never successful, rarely selling more than four hundred copies, a mere fraction of Sower's *Pennsylvanische Berichte* sales. The last known issue is dated December 31, 1757.[18] Isaiah Thomas speaks of Armbruster as a superstitious man who believed in witchcraft and lived in constant fear of attacks from witches. "He imagined that he could, by a special charm, raise or lay the devil; notwithstanding which he was often in great fear and dread of a visit from his Satanic majesty." [19] Armbruster was also convinced that pirate treasures were hidden along the sea coast and the shores of the Delaware and other rivers. Consequently, to the consternation of his employer, he spent much of his time in fruitless searches.

According to Thomas, Armbruster understood copperplate printing, and this would have been sufficient reason for Collins to hire him, for the shop's government work included issues of paper currency printed traditionally from engraved copper plates. Collins was not himself experienced in this method of printing, an intaglio process. A special press with a revolving cylinder, similar to the kind Franklin "contriv'd" to print money in Burlington in 1728, was needed to force the ink out of the etched lines onto the paper. Lawrence C. Wroth maintains that few, if any, letterpress printing houses included copperplate presses, since "the printing of copperplate engravings was a separate industry in this country in the colonial period as it has been, in general, ever since." [20] Collins may have acquired such a press, but it is possible that his issues of paper money were printed for him in another shop.

Printing activity was brisk in 1784 and even more brisk in 1785. No sooner had the compositors and pressmen finished, in 1784, Peter Wilson's compilation of New Jersey laws, from the Declaration of Independence, where Allinson's had left off, to the first sitting of the Council and General Assembly in 1783, than they took on two prestigious assignments. The smaller job was Richard Price's *Observations on the Importance of the American Revolution*, the original of which had been published recently in London. Price, who had been a radical Unitarian minister in the British capital before accepting an invitation from the American government to move to this country in 1778, had acquired a considerable reputation for his political and economic writings. While still in England, Price, a friend of Benjamin Franklin, had attacked his countrymen on the justice and policy of the war in America. His "history" would therefore have been welcomed in the states.[21]

Collins's second historical imprint in 1785, much

bigger than Price's, was David Ramsay's two-volume *History of the Revolution of South-Carolina.* The author was a Philadelphia-trained physician who had lived for several years in Charleston, and at the time of his study he was a delegate to the Continental Congress from his adopted state. He was a temperamental and fastidious writer, but, according to one present-day historian of the Revolution, "he showed unusual insight and a keen sense of proportion . . . in his analysis and interpretation of the events culminating in the Revolution." [22] The manuscript Ramsay gave to Collins, the completion of which preceded by only four years his most remarkable achievement, *The History of the American Revolution,* amounted to six hundred pages, quarto-size.[23]

Ramsay considered the traditional subscription plan undignified and decided to pay for the publication out of his own pocket. Early in 1785 he had thought of giving the assignment to a Philadelphia or London printer. But he settled on Collins, presumably at the suggestion of his father-in-law, Dr. John Witherspoon, president of Princeton College, a man who knew of Collins's fine work.[24]

The job was completed in the early part of December. On Ramsay's optimistic instructions, Collins printed more than three thousand copies to be sold for four dollars a set. It is unfortunate that correspondence which must have gone on between the author and his Trenton printer during 1785 is no longer extant, for of the people Collins worked for or with there was probably none more engaging or more cantankerous than Dr. Ramsay. The printing was done in installments and dragged on all year. Collins, still responsible for the *New-Jersey Gazette* as well as government documents and other regular jobs, could turn out no more than forty pages a week. The fact that Ramsay was ultimately pleased with the typography is expressed in a note in the last chapter of the books, in which he praises Collins as a careful compositor.

In the fall of the year that he worked on Ramsay's history Collins and several other printers, including Shepard Kollock, who was then in New York, bid to reprint the *Journals of Congress* for the sessions since 1777. Among the bidders was Collins's old master, James Adams of Wilmington. However, before Congress acted on the other printers' proposals, John Dunlap of Philadelphia issued an edition of the *Journals* dated 1784–1785. The rest of the bids were immediately dropped. This was the closest Collins came to printing for the federal government.

In 1785 and 1786 Collins was called upon by the state of New Jersey to print blank notes for demands against the forfeited estates of Tories. He also printed handbills notifying persons who had claims on these estates that the notes were ready to be delivered or picked up at the printing shop.[25] Besides doing such routine official work, Collins started in 1787 to issue on a regular basis the convention minutes of the Episcopal Church in New Jersey. He did a private job for John Cleves Symmes, a former legislator, Supreme Court justice, and delegate to Congress, and, in addition, issued copies of the new federal Constitution as agreed to in Philadelphia on September 17.

Collins probably attended the Philadelphia convention of booksellers and printers, held in 1788 to establish regulations for the general benefit of the trade. Benjamin Franklin, aged and feeble, was in attendance.

In 1789 Collins began to relinquish the government

printing he had done without competition in New Jersey for nearly twenty years. Abraham Blauvelt of New Brunswick printed the Votes and Proceedings for that year. Blauvelt, together with the new Burlington printing firm of Isaac Neale and Daniel Lawrence, shared all the legislative work in 1790. Although Collins held the official title of printer to the state through 1795, as of 1789 he had given up most of the government work.

By way of comparison, neighboring Pennsylvania did not have a single "official" government printer. From 1771 to 1776 the printing house of Henry Miller and that of the publishers of the *Pennsylvania Gazette,* David Hall and William Sellers, did most of the Assembly's printing. After 1776 others, such as Melchior Steiner and Charles Cist, Francis Bailey, William and Thomas Bradford, and John Dunlap, also printed for the Assembly.[26]

As a merchant, Collins did business with firms outside the United States, but there is little indication that he engaged extensively in the export trade. On May 4, 1787, he addressed this inquiry to a Philadelphia shipper: "Several Persons residing at this Place who some Time ago Shipped Produce to the House of John Searle and Company of Madeira, having all received their Letters, with an account of Sales, except myself, by the ship Maria, Capt Kollock, I am apprehensive mine must have been mislaid: I will therefore thank thee to make some Enquiry of the Captain or thy clerks whether such a Letter appeared among the Rest on the Ship's last arrival at Philadᵃ." [27]

During the nearly ten years of his estrangement from the Quakers, Collins's interests beyond his shop and his family were generally confined to the Trenton Academy and the Society for Improvement in Useful Knowledge. He was reunited with the Society of Friends in 1787 and afterwards served on numerous committees of the Chesterfield Monthly Meeting, near Trenton, and was a frequent representative to the Quarterly Meeting.

In preparation for the nullification of his disownment, Collins attended the Burlington Monthly Meeting on May 7, 1787, to acknowledge "his error in having acted inconsistently with our peaceable Testimony." [28] He admitted in a paper read before the assemblage that he had been "active in the late War, and" desired "to be reunited in membership with Friends." His statement was "weightily considered, a calm [29] attending the Meeting." He was finally allowed to return to the Society, and three months later his certificate of membership in the Burlington Monthly Meeting arrived at Chesterfield. Since the Burlington Quakers had disowned Collins, it was up to them to return him to membership before he joined the Chesterfield Meeting. In April 1788 the Society took advantage of his experience in helping to establish the Trenton Academy by appointing him to a special committee "to endeavor to promote the establishment of schools." [30] Several years later Collins's worldly experience was again used to consider the subject of spirituous liquors, which, at least until the date of this committee assignment, the printer-merchant sold in his store.

❧ VI ❧

THE COLLINS
BIBLE

By 1789 Isaac Collins had gained a wide reputation
and sufficient experience to undertake the most ambitious project of his career, the production of a King
James Bible, the second quarto edition to be printed
in America. The fact that most Protestant denominations
officially endorsed his venture before the Bible was completed indicates the respect people had for his work.

No Bible in the English language had been printed in
America during the colonial period. There were, how-
ever, Bibles in other tongues. The first to be printed in
America was the Indian Bible, translated by Rev. John
Eliot and printed in Cambridge, Massachusetts, in 1663
by Samuel Green and Marmaduke Johnson. The first
Bible printed in a European language (German) was
issued in 1743 by Christopher Sower of Germantown.

The first English Bible in America was printed in Philadelphia in 1781–82 by Robert Aitken, a long-time business acquaintance of Collins who had issued an English New Testament in 1777. The first American edition of the Roman Catholic Rheims-Douai version was printed by Mathew Carey of Philadelphia in 1790.[1]

Isaiah Thomas, who printed the first volume of his famous folio Bible and also a complete quarto edition in 1791, the same year that Collins printed his, recalled that in his Philadelphia days Collins had earned twenty-five percent higher wages than other journeymen for his "extraordinary attention to business." [2] In a letter to a friend, David Ramsay said: "Though Collins printed the revolution of South Carolina from rather a worse manuscript than Aitkin [sic] has printed the American revolution he has not committed as many errors in the whole two volumes as Aitkin has in many single pages. Aitkins work offends against every principle of good printing." [3]

New Jersey's Governor William Livingston also had a good word for Collins. A year before the printer announced his proposals for publishing the Bible, Livingston wrote: "I have had abundant proof of the accuracy and correctness of his publications, as well as his remarkable attention to business." [4]

Before starting his quarto Bible Collins published four, possibly five, editions of the New Testament. Until 1951, the year George C. Rockefeller, a New Jersey bibliographer, reported his discovery of a 1779 New Testament printed by Collins, it was thought that the first New Jersey Testament bore the date of 1788. In 1899 another bibliographer, William Nelson, listed an edition for 1780, but admitted that he had taken his information from a newspaper advertisement and had not viewed an actual copy of the volume. Rockefeller also reported a 1782 edition printed by Collins.[5] In any event, what must have been the 1779 edition was first advertised in the *New-Jersey Gazette* for March 29, 1780: "A new edition of the New-Testament, Spelling-books, Primers, Parchment, and Writing-Paper, To Be Sold by the Printer hereof." The next notice appeared in the *Gazette* for October 11 and was repeated throughout the rest of the year: "Just Published and to be Sold, wholesale and retail, by Isaac Collins, at the Printing-Office, in Trenton, a neat edition of THE NEW TESTAMENT, Printed in good type, and good paper." In addition to the New Testaments Collins issued in 1779, 1780, and 1782, he published two editions in 1788.

On December 19, 1789, Collins issued an attractive four-page pamphlet setting forth his proposals for printing by subscription "the Holy Bible containing the Old and New Testaments; with the Apocrypha and Marginal Notes." He promised a 984-page quarto volume, reprinted page for page from the Oxford edition and to include an index, a concordance, and assorted tables of measures, weights, and coins used in biblical times.[6] The price to subscribers was set at four Spanish dollars, each roughly the equivalent of 7s. 6d. in the Middle States through the 1780's.[7] As for the mode of payment, the printer stipulated: "One Dollar to be paid at the Time of subscribing, the Remainder on Delivery of the Book."

Relative to this public announcement is a personal letter Collins wrote to Governor Livingston on September 4, 1789, three months before the proposals were made public. It was written in response to Livingston's reaction to Collins's New Testament of 1788 and suggests a possible motive for the printer's desire to publish a complete Bible.

> I received thy Favour respecting the Error in my Edition of the New-Testament, 2d verse of the 10th Chapter of the Hebrews. It is doubtless an Error; but as we copied it from a Cambridge Edition, done under the immediate Authority of the *immaculate* (shall I say) King of Britain, I hold myself less responsible; or at least I hope this Circumstance will be considered as some Explanation [?] of the Blunder. I am well pleased that it claimed thy Attention, and have noted it accordingly. Should other Errors occur, thou wouldst much oblige me by pointing them out also; for I mean to do my best in the Quarto Edition of the Bible, which I expect to begin this Fall. It would be very agreeable to me if I could have thy Assistance in Reading the Proof-Sheets; but if thou wert willing to take the Trouble I do not see how I ——— at it.
>
> It is much to be regretted there were not more Readers of these excellent Writings, the Scriptures—honest Readers —Searchers after Truth. But alas! the World in general are become too wise to seek information in these holy Writings—and, what is most to be lamented is, that those especially who are Men of Letters, and those who ought to know better, are generally the most delinquent. What is the Cause? Is it not that the *Temple* is too much occupied, as in old Time, with those who sell Oxen and Sheep and Doves—and where are the Changers of Money sitting? [8]

The publication and sale of books by subscription developed from the system of individual patronage of authors. "It is in effect the exchange of the single patron for the many, the single patron, with his indefinite assurance of aid, for the many, with their pledges to purchase upon publication, at a fixed price, one or more copies of a proposed book." [9] This procedure, which David Ramsay thought undignified, was of extraordinary importance in the marketing of books in the eighteenth century. Collins simply adopted the plan he had employed in publishing two separate compilations of New Jersey laws, one in 1776 and the other in 1784.[10]

Risking no financial loss, despite his personal determination, Collins insisted that the printing of the Bible would be started as soon as 3,000 copies had been reserved by subscribers, the book "to be finished without Delay." However, subscriptions did not come in as quickly as he had expected. Sometime between the initial announcement of December 1789 and the completion of the Bible Collins tried to attract more subscribers by agreeing to include John Downame's *Concordance* in the bound volume without increasing the original price. He said subscribers were far short of the number proposed but that he had made up his mind "to risk such a Number of Copies as he apprehends will be sufficient to cover all the Subscriptions that may be obtained." [11] Collins's optimism is to be admired, but seldom in the middle eighteenth century did presses average much more than 300 to 500 copies of a book. One exception was Benjamin Franklin's *Poor Richard's Almanack,* 9,771 copies of which he and David Hall printed and sold in 1766.[12] Another exception, of course, was the Bible, the popularity of which Collins must have counted on, in view of the fact that his was to be the first printed in New Jersey and only the second of its kind in the country.

Before Aitken's Bible there had been other efforts to publish English editions in America, but the sparseness of the colonial population and the attendant mechanical difficulties of printing such a large work precluded their publication. "Bibles, however, were imported freely from England and Holland, but when the colonies declared their independence, the matter soon became serious. Books could not be so easily imported, and there soon followed a general destitution of Bibles, as well as other books, which was keenly felt." [13] So acute was the shortage and the believed need that the Continental Congress in 1777 resolved to import 20,000 copies of the Bible. This was never done, but Aitken published an edition of the New Testament, followed by three more editions in 1778, 1779, and 1781, two years before Collins issued his first New Testaments.

Encouraged by the reception of these editions of the New Testament, Aitken announced his proposals to publish the whole Bible, and successfully petitioned Congress to adopt the following resolution: "That the United States in Congress assembled, highly approve the pious and laudable undertaking of Mr. Aitken [and] they recommend this edition of the Bible to the inhabitants of the United States, and hereby authorize him to publish this recommendation in the manner he shall think proper." [14]

One important difference between the production of Aitken's Bible and the production of Collins's is that in 1782 the war was still not settled and Aitken was forced to work under conditions much less propitious than those existing for the New Jersey printer several years later. As a writer in the *Freeman's Journal,* a Philadelphia publication, said in 1781: ". . . the whole book is . . . purely American, and has risen, like the fabled Phoenix, from the ashes of that pile in which our enemies supposed they had consumed the liberties of America." [15] Also, in relation to Collins's cautious subscription plan, Aitken is said to have lost "more than three thousand pounds specie" due to the costly circumstances of production. Collins, we may assume, was not willing to suffer a similar embarrassment.[16] It is also interesting to note that Collins's decision to publish a "purely American" Bible came at about the same time Congress denied Aitken the exclusive right to print Bibles in this country for fourteen years.[17] A new enterprise had been opened to the book-publishing industry, and Collins was among the first to seize the opportunity.

Collins's printed proposals included extracts from the minutes of various religious denominations which endorsed his project. The pamphlet also contained a specimen of the type and paper to be used in the Bible, and also a blank form on which subscribers could sign up for copies. Copies of this pamphlet were distributed in most of the states in order to get the widest possible coverage among printers, booksellers, and churchmen. In Philadelphia subscriptions were solicited by Joseph Crukshank, Collins's former partner, and William Young. Edmund Prior and Samuel Loudon solicited New Yorkers, and in Boston David West and Ebenezer Larkin were the printer's agents. Joseph Townsend sought subscribers in Baltimore.

Most of Collins's support, however, came from the religious groups. On the last page of his proposals Collins printed an appeal to the sects: "The Editor . . . wishes to attract the Attention, and obtain the Countenance of People of ALL Denominations in this arduous

Undertaking." Early in the Bible's planning stage the printer was able to win, first, the support of the Society of Friends, but also substantial encouragement from the Presbyterians, the Episcopalians, and the Baptists.

At the Meeting for Sufferings in Philadelphia on March 19, 1789, the Quakers recommended to the Quarterly and Monthly Meetings of the Philadelphia Yearly Meeting that they appoint committees to assist Collins in obtaining subscriptions. By October the clerk of the Chesterfield Meeting, of which Collins was a member, reported that he had received money for twenty-three Bibles, a substantial number for that comparatively small group.[18] Typical of the general cooperation among Quakers was the decision by the Meeting for Sufferings of the New England Yearly Meeting, held on April 1, 1789, to recommend that individual monthly meetings "appoint suitable persons to promote and receive Subscriptions agreeable to the tenor of said proposals." The meeting also decided to act as a collection agency for subscriptions in New England. Collins was authorized to print the endorsement as part of his proposals.[19]

The Presbyterians, at a meeting of their general assembly on May 25, 1789, in Philadelphia, appointed a number of delegates "to lay Mr. Collins's Proposals before their respective Presbyteries; and to recommend to them, by Order of the General Assembly, that a Person or Persons be appointed in every Congregation . . . to procure Subscriptions." [20]

The Presbyterians, whose enthusiasm and assistance in "every Congregation" must have heightened Collins's own enthusiasm, further appointed, through their New

York and New Jersey Synod, a three-man committee to help the printer revise and correct proof sheets. The clergymen were Dr. John Witherspoon and Dr. Samuel Stanhope Smith, presidents in succession of the College of New Jersey, and John F. Armstrong, clerk of the general assembly. In following years, these Calvinists reaffirmed their endorsement, "that it be recommended to every presbytery and every individual of this assembly, to make returns of all subscriptions made for this purpose. . . ." [21]

The Episcopalians were next to endorse the Collins Bible. At the Convention of the Protestant Episcopal Church in Philadelphia on August 8, 1789, they resolved: "That the Members of this Convention will assist Mr. Collins in the procuring of Subscriptions." [22] Rev. John Cox, of St. John's in Trenton, a personal friend of Collins, had been a leader in the June endorsement by New Jersey Episcopalians at their state convention in Elizabethtown. He also urged other states to follow suit.

The Baptists made known their receptiveness to Collins's project at their Philadelphia convention in October. They were more explicit in what they expected of this new edition of the Bible. Like the Presbyterians, they appointed a committee to help Collins with revisions and corrections, but instructed the committee to try to prevent the inclusion of the Apocrypha, "or any Notes of any Kind," for such they believed would have "a dangerous Tendency to corrupt the Simplicity and Truth of the sacred Scriptures." [23]

The Presbyterians had been somewhat skeptical of Collins's decision to include as part of the finished volume

Jean Frederic Ostervald's scholarly *Practical Observations on the Old and New Testaments*. However, they consented to go along with the printer and the other denominational committees. Their Calvinist heritage had been relaxed "in such Manner as may best promote the Publication." [24]

Nevertheless, Collins took note of the debate and printed in his proposals the following compromise:

> Finding a Variety of Sentiments respecting the Apocrypha and any Notes on the Text, the Editor informs the Publick, that he is desirous to comply with the Wishes of every Subscriber, as well as with the Directions of the Committees of different Denominations on this Head;— Subscribers, therefore, upon timely Notice, shall be supplied with Books containing either the Apocrypha or Ostervald's Notes, or both, or neither—as they choose. —In this Situation the Editor is under the absolute Necessity of throwing Ostervald's Notes at the End of the Book, subject to such additional Expense as shall be agreed upon by the Committee hereafter mentioned.[25]

Such reluctance on the part of some denominations to accept the Apocrypha or any interpretation of the Scriptures, even by the noted French minister of Switzerland, probably came as no surprise to Collins. For one thing, it was often a Friend's misfortune to be accused by other Protestants of slighting the Bible. But the printer wanted to make his edition of the Bible complete and attractive for as many potential subscribers as possible.[26]

Collins came as close as he probably hoped in realizing the "Countenance of People of ALL Denominations." What remained, in addition to the actual labor of printing and binding his "arduous Undertaking," was the final endorsement of the interdenominational committee. Besides Witherspoon, Smith, and Armstrong for the Presbyterians, other signers of the statement were Oliver Hart, Samuel Jones, and Burgiss Allison for the Baptists. Their statement of approval is dated August 1790:

> The Underwritten have examined the edition of the Holy Scriptures which Mr. Isaac Collins of Trenton is publishing, as far as he has proceeded—are highly satisfied with the neatness and accuracy of the work—and believe that in the critical attention paid to the different editions of England and Scotland, to the difference of words which are to be found in these editions, and to the care bestowed upon the execution of the whole, the work will be equal to any in the English language.[27]

By September 1791, nearly two years after the first public announcements of his proposals, Collins's Bible had grown from an expected 984 pages to the final 1,150, made bulkier by Downame's *Concordance*. On September 1 the printer released a broadside together with a general newspaper notice promising subscribers that the book would be finished by October 1, and although it may be reasonable to assume that some copies were issued to subscribers on that date, there is no evidence that he was able to keep his promise. In a notice that first appeared in the *Pennsylvania Gazette* on January 11, 1792, Collins reported that the Bible was "in the hands of several binders—and when the books are ready for delivery, subscribers will be notified where to call or send for them." The notice continued to appear in the *Gazette,* Collins's regular medium of advertising in Philadelphia, until April 18, which suggests that subscribers had begun to receive their copies.[28]

Meanwhile, Collins's famous competitor as the publisher of the first quarto King James Bible in America, Isaiah Thomas of Worcester, Massachusetts, had also run behind schedule. In a notice dated September 29, 1791, inserted in the October 19 edition of the *Pennsylvania Journal, and the Weekly Advertiser,* Thomas's favorite Philadelphia paper, he reported "this day completed the Old and New Testaments of his Royal Quarto Edition of the Holy Bible." He said that the Apocrypha and the index had yet to be finished but that he anticipated all would be done by the last day of November. But it was not until December 22 that Thomas was finally able to advertise in his own *Massachusetts Spy: or, the Worcester Gazette,* "The Royal Quarto Bible...is THIS DAY [December 15] completed from the Press." In the same edition of the *Spy* the printer notified subscribers to his folio Bible that the printing of the first volume was completed the same day, "and will be put in boards, with all speed. Subscribers may be supplied...in fourteen days from this date...." However, Thomas's September notice continued to appear in Philadelphia papers until March 21, 1792, a month before Collins's advertisements ceased to appear in that city.[29]

What all this suggests is that neither Collins nor Thomas was able to issue bound copies of the Bible in 1791, the date that appears on the title pages of both editions. This was not unusual, for printers seldom were able to keep exact schedules. For such a large undertaking as a complete quarto Bible Collins and Thomas may well have been hampered by short supplies of type, slow proofreading, problems with engravings (in

Thomas's case), and the scarcity of paper and leather. In any event, their race was a close one, with Thomas apparently the winner by a month or so. One other point of interest is the slight difference in size between the two Bibles. Thomas's was a "Royal Quarto"—8¾ x 11¾ inches—and Collins's a regular quarto—8¼ x 10½ inches.

In place of the traditional dedication to King James, Collins published an address, or essay, "To the Reader," by Dr. John Witherspoon. The first paragraph is worth reproducing for its polite repudiation of Great Britain, which in the early days had restricted printing of the Bible in America. "As the Dedication of the English translation of the BIBLE to king James the first of England seems to be wholly unnecessary for the purposes of edification, and perhaps on some accounts improper to be continued in an American edition, the Editor has been advised by some judicious friends to omit it, and to prefix to this edition a short account of the translations of the Old and New Testaments from the original Hebrew and Greek in which they were written." The commentary thereafter appeared in editions of the Bible by other American printers for a period of thirty years.[30] Collins noted in the preface, or "advertisement," to the second edition, which was published in New York in 1806–07, that Mathew Carey, William Durrell, and other printers adopted the 1791 edition as their standard of correctness. The printer also identified Dr. Witherspoon, whose name did not appear in the 1791 edition, as the author of the introductory commentary. The care taken by Collins is evident from the closing paragraph of the commentary:

The Publisher has only further to add, that he has made
the following impression from the Oxford edition of 1784
by Jackson and Hamilton—and has been particularly
attentive in the revisal and correction of the proof-sheets
with the Cambridge edition of 1668 by John Field—with
the Edinburgh edition of 1775 by Kincaid, and, in all
variations, with the London edition of 1772 by Eyre and
Strahan—that where there was any difference in words,
or in the omission or addition of words, among these, he
followed that which appeared to be most agreeable to the
Hebrew of Arias Montanus, and to the Greek of Arias
Montanus and Leusden, without permitting himself to de-
part from some one of the above-mentioned English copies,
unless in the mode of spelling, in which he has generally
followed Johnson.[31]

The Bible was "well bound," as Collins had promised
in his proposals pamphlet and subsequent advertisements.
Though bookbinding by the 1790's had become a highly
decorative art in America, Collins's Bible, like most of
the books he produced, was plainly bound. It is hard to
tell how many different binders he hired for the job, but
the Wilmington firm of Craig and Lea bound a quantity
in sprinkled sheep, simply adorned on the front and back
by blind fillets. A binder's label, or "ticket," inside the
cover of a copy in the Library of Congress identifies the
Wilmington binders. Plain endpapers are glued on the
insides of the boards, but two marks of superior work-
manship stand out—raised cords and silk headbands. The
cords, laced into the covers to create attractive ridges
across the spine, indicate great care on the part of the
binders. Headbands, mainly for show, were sewn onto the
top and bottom of the spine. "Careful binders said that
a book should no more be seen in a library without head-

bands than a gentleman should appear in public minus a collar." [32]

Two copies owned by Rutgers University Library clearly were bound by different shops. One, whose binder is identified by a ticket as Philip Weaver of Germantown, has a two-line fillet around the edges of the calf covers, five raised cords with gold floral decoration, and the word "Bible" in gold on a red morocco spine panel outlined by a gold floral pattern. The second copy, whose binder is not identified, has a simple double-line border with an elaborate blind-tooled center pattern forming two boxes, or panels. The cords are raised, but if gold tooling was used it is no longer visible on the calf.

On at least one occasion we know of Collins contracted James Muir and George Hyde of Philadelphia to bind one copy of the quarto Bible in two volumes. For what must have been a special customer, or subscriber, the order called for morocco, gilt leaves, and gold tooling on the spine and covers. According to the receipted invoice from Muir and Hyde, now in the Stewart Collection of the Glassboro State College Library, Glassboro, New Jersey, Collins paid the large sum of £4 10s.

Collins's Bible was an immediate success. Four-fifths of the first printing, which he increased to five thousand, eventually were purchased by the Society of Friends. Tradition has it that Joseph Crukshank of Philadelphia, for one, could not sell any other quarto Bibles after Collins's became available.[33]

Hugh Gaine, by this time the dean of New York printers, entered the field in 1792 with what is believed to be the first printing of the Bible in that city. Gaine's edition, however, is said to have been set in type in Scotland and shipped to the United States. About the same time another New York firm, Hodge and Campbell, issued an edition fully composed in that city.[34]

Publication of the King James version thereafter spread rapidly in the United States. More than twenty editions of the complete Bible and more than forty of the New Testament were published before 1800. Of the Bibles, ten were published in Philadelphia, seven in Worcester, Massachusetts, two in Trenton, and three in New York. Of the New Testaments, sixteen appeared in Philadelphia, four or five from Collins's press in Trenton, five in Wilmington, four in New Haven, three in Lancaster, Pennsylvania, three in Boston, two in New York, two in Newburyport, Massachusetts, and two in Exeter, New Hampshire.[35] James Adams, Collins's former master, had issued the first New Testament in Delaware in 1781, and Shepard Kollock printed an edition in Elizabethtown, New Jersey, in 1788. In addition, another close friend, Joseph Crukshank, began printing Testaments in 1782 and issued the first American edition of John Wesley's version in 1791. Archibald Bartram, a nephew, published a New Testament in Philadelphia in 1799.

Biblical scholars have long referred to Collins's Bible as one of the most correct editions. Great care was taken in its preparation. A copy of the Cambridge edition which Collins followed to correct the proof sheets was loaned to him by its owner, a Princeton mathematician. The printer turned to Rev. John F. Armstrong for advice on the Hebrew and Greek texts. A Trenton clergyman, Armstrong had worked with Collins in developing the Trenton Academy. Several of Collins's children examined the proofs as many as eleven times, and received one pound for each error they detected. They missed a broken letter, a misplaced punctuation mark, and *thy* doctrine for *the* doctrine in I Timothy 4:16.

As sales of the Bible rose, Collins, like other Bible publishers, issued a smaller, octavo, edition in 1793 and 1794. It did not include the extensive index or Downame's *Concordance*. The reason for the two dates on the title page is that Collins printed the Old Testament in 1793 and the New Testament in 1794, sometimes binding the latter separately in a less expensive cover. He published a second edition of the 1791 Bible from his New York shop in 1806–07, his final imprint before retiring from business. However, his firm issued a third edition sometime after 1813.

Aside from the Testaments and the Bible, few significant volumes were issued from Collins's Trenton presses between 1790 and 1795. But of the activity in his shop in the latter year we are fortunate to know a great deal. In Collins's personal copy of a pocket almanac, *Poor Will's Almanack for the Year 1795,* now in the library at Rutgers University, are recorded a number of his business transactions.[36]

By 1795, Collins had probably made his decision to move to New York; however, the printing office bustled with trade. From February through most of December 1795 the firm issued a number of titles, from Bibles and religious tracts to spelling books and state laws, totaling more than three thousand single bound volumes. Preeminent among these were Lindley Murray's *The Power of Religion on the Mind* and *The Life of Sarah Grubb,* the latter being an anonymously edited anthology of a late Quaker missionary's writings. As late as November Collins was also sending printed sheets of his octavo Bible to binders, sheets which no doubt had been stored after printing and bound piecemeal as customers demanded them.

Among the book dealers who purchased copies of both the quarto and octavo Bibles were John Dickins (or Dickens), a Philadelphia bookseller of predominantly Methodist imprints, William Wilson, also of Philadelphia, and Edmund Prior of New York. Collins also continued to work closely with his former partner, Crukshank. On September 13 he sent fifty octavo Bibles to Crukshank "to replace," as Collins put it, "those I borrowed of him last Winter or Spring." On November 28 he sent Crukshank "by Capt Ashmore 514 Borgois Text and 50 Pica Do. in 11 Bundles." [37] This exchange with Crukshank illustrates how early American printers solved the problem of the general scarcity of type. Not only was type scarce, but it was expensive, and few printers could afford to stock all varieties. Further, without adequate supplies of type, author and printer of a long book were often hampered in completing the proofreading and making corrections before the type set for early chapters had to be distributed for use in succeeding chapters.

In 1795 Collins helped Archibald Bartram and Stacy Budd, relatives of his wife, obtain a loan from the Pemberton family in Philadelphia, to be used for the purchase of a font of type for an edition of Alexander Cruden's popular *Biblical Concordance*. Bartram, who had served Collins as an apprentice, had joined Budd in forming a publishing and merchandising business in Philadelphia, and they issued a few imprints during the next few years.

Throughout the year Philip Weaver in Germantown received a large portion of the bindery work from the Collins shop. Also contracted were George Hyde of Philadelphia and James Wilson of Wilmington.

Collins used two local shipping companies in 1795, and presumably in other years. Usually his shipper across and down the Delaware to Philadelphia and Wilmington was Captain Thomas Ashmore of Trenton. For shipments toward New York and other points in the east, Collins employed the wagons and boats of Colonel John Neilson, a New Brunswick merchant. Colonel Neilson, a respected army officer during the war, had served New Jersey as a delegate to the Continental Congress. He had known Collins for several years, and he subscribed regularly to the *New-Jersey Gazette* and donated liberally to the Trenton Academy building fund.[38]

Collins's letter to a Philadelphia bookseller, William Young, reveals the frustrations that confronted the eighteenth-century printer who depended upon the crude and frequently unreliable methods of transportation of the times: "I wrote thee a few Days ago for an Assortment of Children's Books—If they should not be sent off before this gets to Hand I should be glad they could come by the Bearer James Kirkpatrick instead of the Stage— they will be more likely to come safe and cost less freight." [39]

Sometime in the summer or fall of 1796 Collins and his wife Rachel packed their many belongings and moved their family to New York. Little is known about the family's departure from Trenton. We do know that Collins himself stayed on long enough to print the Votes and Proceedings of the second sitting of the General

Assembly. A letter the printer sent on March 4, 1796, to Assembly Speaker Ebenezer Elmer mentions this assignment:

> I have at length completed the Printing of the Votes and Proceedings of the general Assembly of the last Sitting, and they will be folded and served in a few days, and delivered to the Treasurer. Nothing has delayed the Work so long but the Difficulty of procuring the Paper. I travelled upwards of 200 Miles among Papermills in Pursuit of it, and was finally obliged to wait till it was made by Special Contract. This Information I thought would be right for me to give, lest the Delay should be attributed to a wrong Cause.
>
> But *four pounds* per Sheet is not Sufficient—is not a reasonable Compensation. For an individual I would not have done it for less than five pounds, when the *Necessities of Life* were much less in Price than they are now: I want the Legislature therefore to agree to pay me *five pounds* per Sheet for the Work I am now completing, as well as for the Votes of the present Sitting.—If my Proposition should be likely to obtain, it can be brought forward by a Motion; otherwise I do not wish anything to appear on the Minutes, and which is the Reason I have not preferred a formal Petition.[40]

Collins's request to increase the charge for printing a sheet in folio from £4 to £5 failed, for the receipted bill from James Mott, the treasurer, quotes eighty shillings New Jersey currency, the equivalent of £4, as the amount Collins received. The total payment was £66 for sixteen and a half sheets.[41]

Collins's charges to the New Jersey legislature for work done in 1796 may be compared with those by Timothy Green to the Connecticut Assembly for printing the collected laws of 1784, despite the difference of twelve years.⁴² Green's charge of forty shillings Connecticut currency for a sheet in folio, four pages to the sheet, was half that charged by Collins. The difference is explained partly by the fact that Connecticut money had not depreciated as much as New Jersey money during the postwar period. Another reason is that the cost of paper after the war had risen fourteen to twenty shillings a ream from what it had been in the 1760's and 1770's. Further evidence of the difference in printing prices between Connecticut and New Jersey is James Parker's charge of £3 per octavo sheet for printing Samuel Smith's *History of . . . New Jersey* in 1765 in Woodbridge, New Jersey. By comparison, Collins's charge more than thirty years later does not appear exorbitant. When one considers the printer's profit needed to absorb such things as equipment deterioration, lost time of workmen, and other overhead items, Collins's charge, whether £4 or £5 a sheet, seems to be in line with existing printing prices.

The "present Sitting" to which Collins referred in the second paragraph of the letter to Elmer was the second sitting of the Assembly's twentieth session, which convened in Trenton in June 1796—not to be confused with "the Work I am now completing" for the nineteenth session. The Votes and Proceedings of this second sitting of the twentieth session was Isaac Collins's final New Jersey imprint.

⤙ VII ⤚
A FAMILY
BUSINESS

"It was indeed a favor to move our little ones so great a distance without any injury or accident," Rachel Collins wrote to her sister, Elizabeth Bartram, wife of the Philadelphia druggist, Moses, in November 1796. She complained, however, of the "musketoes" that "cruelly treated" little Mary, seven, and the baby Joseph, two. "Mary was recovering when I got there, but poor Joseph was attacked the first night and in a few days he looked as if he had the small pox very bad—he scratched the bites and they festered and inflamed so much that he could get little sleep and had it continued I question whether he would have survived many more bites, but, at this time he is better and looks an altered child, is bravely as to health except a cough." [1]

The nine other children who had made the trip to New

York with their parents were Sarah, aged twenty-one; Elizabeth, nineteen; Thomas, seventeen; Susannah, fifteen; William, fourteen; Benjamin, twelve; Anna, ten; Isaac, Jr., eight; and Stacy, five. Rebecca, the eldest, now twenty-four, and Charles, two years younger, had already taken up residence there. Charles, an apprentice to Robert Bowne, prominent Quaker printer and merchant on Pearl Street, doubled as his father's sales representative in New York. Another child, named for her mother, had died in infancy in 1778.

The Collinses had shipped their personal belongings and printing equipment by boat from Philadelphia. Rachel explained to her sister that they had expected the items to arrive only a day or two after the family's arrival. Instead, it was seventeen days from the time the vessel set off before it arrived at the port of New York. "Thee may imagine how very anxious we were and fearfull she had foundered at sea; however she came at last without any damage, to the joy of the whole family and I hope a degree of thankfulness to Him who rules the stormy ocean and at His command the raging sea is still." [2]

Finally settled in their home and shop at 189 Pearl Street, the Collinses arranged to have their membership in the Chesterfield Monthly Meeting transferred to the New York Monthly Meeting. The certificate of transfer for Isaac, Rachel, and nine of their children is dated November 8, 1796, the other four members of the family having transferred at an earlier time. Charles's certificate, for example, is dated December 4, 1792, about the time his apprenticeship to Robert Bowne became effective.[3] There is some question as to which meeting house they attended, since two existed in the city, one on old Crown Street and the other on Queen Street, which today is an extension of Pearl Street.

The original Crown Street meeting house, the first in New York, was built in 1748 and used during the Revolution as a British hospital. In 1794 it was torn down and a new one was constructed on nearly the same site. Considering that its congregation was older and that it was closer to their home, it is likely that this was the meeting house Collins and his family usually attended. The Queen Street house, called the "New Quaker Meeting," was a handsome brick structure built in 1775.[4] In a city dominated by Episcopal, Dutch Reformed, and Presbyterian congregations, the Quakers were not as influential as they were in the Philadelphia area, but they were foremost in promoting charitable and humanitarian undertakings of a nonsectarian nature.[5] Collins and members of his family were active in a number of these community projects.

The city of New York had recently replaced Philadelphia as the largest city in the United States. In 1790, the year the national capital was moved to Philadelphia, New York's population was more than 33,000, compared with Philadelphia's 28,500. The other centers of population and commerce were Baltimore, Boston, and Charleston. New York by 1796 had grown to almost 60,000 persons, and, according to one foreign visitor, it was the "most agreeable as well as the most flourishing city in the United States."[6] To Isaac Collins, whose decision to leave Burlington in 1778 was based on the apparent future of Trenton, the city of New York nearly twenty years later must have appeared to be the most promising

American city of all in which to dwell and carry on commercial activity.

The growth of New York was stimulated by the steady flow of immigrants and other newcomers from New England and the Middle Atlantic states after the war. Colonel Richard Varick was mayor when Collins moved there, and Aaron Burr and Alexander Hamilton were powerful political leaders. Noah Webster, the prominent Connecticut author and lawyer, and Thomas Greenleaf, a newspaper publisher, had come to the city, and also the inventor John Fitch and the artist John Trumbull. Lindley Murray, the noted grammarian, had only recently moved from New York to England, and Collins remained one of his American publishers. James Rivington and Hugh Gaine, formerly the leading Loyalist newspaper editors, had abandoned their papers, and in the 1790's they operated book and stationery stores on Pearl Street. Gaine also devoted some time to job printing.[7]

Along Pearl Street were the newspaper publishers John Lang, Archibald McLean, and John Tiebout. Lang and McLean, located at No. 116, published the *New York Gazette and General Advertiser,* and Tiebout issued the *Tablet; and Weekly Advertiser* from his shop at No. 358. In the same neighborhood was John Bull, editor of the *Sentimental and Literary Magazine.* The paper in which Collins regularly advertised was Webster's *Herald; A Gazette for the Country,* published about six blocks away on Pine Street, near Wall Street.

The *Herald* (renamed the *Spectator* late in 1797) was established in 1794 as a semiweekly rural newspaper, an offshoot of Webster's daily *American Minerva; and Evening Advertiser,* which he had started the previous year

as a political organ. The *Herald,* essentially an abridgement of the parent publication, circulated in the outskirts
of the city proper, where a number of Quaker families
lived. Since many of Collins's imprints, as well as other
volumes stocked in his bookstore, were written by
Quakers, the *Herald* was the printer's most likely medium
of advertising. The *American Minerva* was renamed in
1797 also, becoming the *Commercial Advertiser.* Webster, who later abandoned journalism to become America's
pioneer lexicographer, was an articulate spokesman for
the Federalist program because, for one thing, he thought
it was ridiculous for an author to have to copyright his
literary property in each of the thirteen states. While in
New York, he received encouragement in his newspaper
enterprises from Alexander Hamilton, just as Aaron
Burr, Hamilton's political rival, supported *Greenleaf's
New-York Journal,* the opposition paper.

Collins did not have to go far from his Pearl Street
address for printing supplies. The street itself was a bee-
hive of merchandising activity. William Durell, for instance, at 208 Pearl Street, could have supplied printing
paper. John Roberts, the engraver, had his shop at 136
Pearl Street. Several years after Collins's arrival, an ink-
maker, John Bowen, moved to Pearl from Frankfort
Street. Besides Collins, Gaine, and Rivington, several
printers, booksellers, and stationers maintained shops on
Pearl Street. So great was their concentration by 1797
that a bookbinder, Peter Mesier, opened a shop only a
few doors from Collins's place.

In David Longworth's city directory for 1796 Collins
and his son Charles are listed simply as merchants, and in
a separate line the father is also listed as a printer. But

their main business at this time was dry goods. They shared the Pearl Street address. In September 1797, when they began advertising in the *Herald,* the Collins firm, "near the Fly-Market," proclaimed the arrival from Europe of a large assortment of dry goods, "suitable for the approaching season, which they will sell on low terms for cash, short credit, or country produce." The partners also noted that they had some used printing type for sale.[8]

What may have influenced the father to join his son in the dry goods business was the growth of the textile industry in New York following the war. And very likely, the Collinses were encouraged by the city's rising export-import trade, which at the end of the 1790's had increased to nearly ten times that of the beginning.[9] Charles presumably had charge of the dry goods store, while his father ran the printing shop. The dry goods business probably never amounted to much, for in 1799 the firm was appraised at $2,000, in contrast to that of their friend and neighbor Edmund Prior, whose business at 261 Pearl Street was worth $15,000.[10] The elder Collins commented in his will that his son was "unsuccessful in trade." [11]

In this environment, and in a time propitious for commercial success, Collins, in his fiftieth year, began the final phase of his business career. His only New York printing assignment in 1796 was a small instructional book on baptism, but in 1797, his first full year in the city, business picked up. With the publication of sermons by William Savery and George Dillwyn and Job Scott's *Journal,* Collins became one of the principal printers of Quaker literature in New York. His bookstore, however, was stocked not only with Quaker imprints but also with writings on the doctrines and disciplines of most other denominations. The Savery and Dillwyn sermons, printed and bound together in a single volume, were instructive about the ministry of these two preachers in Europe during 1796–98. Savery, "one of the most renowned public Friends of the post-Revolutionary period," [12] was much read and a popular preacher. He believed that his ministry was particularly effective when directed toward persons outside the Society of Friends. Yet he did not knowingly seek converts; outsiders, he thought, could benefit from his preaching without leaving their own sects.[13] Dillwyn, a long-time friend of the Collins family, was not as well known as Savery, although his sermons were also in demand.

Religious controversy surrounded the publication of Scott's *Journal*. A spokesman for Quaker quietism, the inward experience of God, Scott's views were closely akin to those of Elias Hicks, leader of the society's so-called liberal faction. After Scott's death in 1793 during a religious visit to Ireland his journal and other papers were brought before the New England Yearly Meeting for possible publication. Hicks' biographer gives this interpretation of the proceedings: "This body had already issued two of his works, but before the *Journal* could be edited the thinking of the Yearly Meeting had so changed that it first hesitated and then refused to sanction the printing of the *Journal* of its most famous liberal." [14] Theological views within the society were changing at the time; for example, there was a growing evangelical trend in opposition to liberalism.[15] Meanwhile, the Meeting for Sufferings of the New York Yearly Meeting, influenced by Hicks, acquired a copy of Scott's manuscript and Collins contracted to publish it in a quarto volume of 360 pages. It is interesting to note that a leader of the evangelical movement was Stephen Grellet, who in 1804 married Rebecca Collins.

Scott's *Journal,* like the many other published accounts of Quaker ministry, sold well. Collins issued two editions in 1797 and printed the fourth in 1798. In the latter year the old New York Typographical Society reorganized and was renamed the Franklin Typographical Society. By 1799 it had fifty members.[16] This revival of the Society was indicative of New York's position as a major center of printing and publishing following the war. Between 1790 and 1820 it attracted nearly forty typefounders for varying periods of time, and about thirty copperplate printers operated in the city during the same period. They had been particularly trained in the printing of maps, portraits, book plates, billheads, paper money, and certificates of membership. About eight printers had shops within an area of a few blocks on either side of Collins's Pearl Street establishment, not to mention the dozens of others located on other business streets.[17]

Collins's printing of Scott's *Journal* led in 1798 to his proposals for printing by subscription George Fox's *Journal* in two large volumes. An historical account by the founder of the Society of Friends, the *Journal* was first published in 1694, three years after Fox's death. It is the simple narrative of his spiritual experiences and of the persecution to which he and his followers were subjected by the authorities in England. By January 1799 Collins had not yet received half of the thousand subscriptions "indispensably necessary to make it worth while to put the work to press." [18] The book was finally published a year later.

As he had done in Trenton, Collins occasionally issued imprints expressly for booksellers who had copyright privileges but did not have their own printing equipment. Such was his relationship at least on one occasion with the New York bookseller Cornelius Davis. In 1799 Collins was among several printers, including his old friend Shepard Kollock of Elizabethtown, New Jersey, who printed for Davis the multivolume *History of Jacobinism,* a French work in translation. Collins printed the third volume and Kollock printed the fourth. Printing assignments of this nature are evidence of Collins's high reputation as a careful craftsman and a dependable and efficient businessman.

Among Collins's other imprints in 1799 were a twelve-page pamphlet by Fénelon, two sermons in a larger book by John Henry Livingston, a collection of New York penal laws, and, most important, Lindley Murray's *English Reader,* an anthology of prose and poetry "from the Best Writers." Murray, whose *English Grammar* of 1795 enjoyed phenomenal popularity (Collins issued the third edition in 1800), had moved to England from New York almost immediately after the war. His New York estate, Bellevue, was acquired by the city in 1798 and became the site years later of Bellevue Hospital. His books were particularly acceptable to the Society of Friends, "as they were composed to animate piety and goodness and lacked appeal for the corrupt mind." [19]

So important was the printing of Murray's *Grammar* to the Collins shop that it was the only job Rachel mentioned in a letter to her youngest daughter, Mary. "Tell thy brother Isaac not to be discouraged from writing because Tommy has not answered his letter, for he is a good deal engaged in the printing office—we are printing Lindley Murray's large grammar which will be finished and ready for sale in a few weeks." [20] Mary and Isaac, Jr. were at the time enrolled in a boarding school, while Thomas, having turned twenty-one on March 3, 1800, had joined his brother Charles and his father in the family business.

The year 1800 also marked the firm's first effort at printing a medical book, Dr. Valentine Seaman's *Midwives Monitor, and Mothers Mirror*. The work was an outgrowth of a series of lectures Dr. Seaman presented for midwives in 1798 at the New York Hospital nursing school that he had helped to establish. Seaman, a Quaker, was perhaps best known for his pioneer work with cowpox vaccine to immunize against smallpox. After the death of his child in the New York smallpox epidemic of 1796, he visited Dr. Edward Jenner in England to learn about this vaccination technique.[21] Seaman, like some of his contemporaries, attributed the cause of yellow fever, a recurring New York problem, to uncleanliness rather than to some organism. Nearly a century passed, however, before scientists were convinced that it was mosquito-borne.

Fever epidemics had struck New York both in 1798 and 1799, but, as Rachel reported the next year in her letter to Mary, "not a single case of the yellow fever is believed to be here which is cause of thankfulness to the Almighty dispenser of every good." [22] In the following years, however, the dreaded disease returned, reaching such epidemic proportions in 1805 that the Collins family was forced to spend most of the year at their country home in West Farms, Westchester County, about twelve miles from the city. Despite the move Rachel contracted the disease and died on September 15 at the age of fifty-five. "We had no Suspicion of her Disorder being the yellow fever till near the Close," Isaac wrote to the Bartrams in Philadelphia, "and the Doctor who was, as a Physician, her favorite, was, I believe as ignorant as ourselves. So mild a Case it is tho't seldom ever occured. The fear of Death that she dreaded exceedingly when well, was entirely taken away." [23]

For more than thirty-four years Rachel Collins had worked with her husband; together they had built successful publishing enterprises in three cities, and together they had reared a large family. "I feel ruined and wholly undone," Isaac said in the letter to Moses and Elizabeth Bartram. "She was so lovely—every Thing to me. She was indeed the Crown and Diadem of our Family."

In April, only a few months before Rachel's death, Benjamin D. Perkins had joined Isaac and Thomas as a full "copartner" and at about the same time Charles left the business to form a separate firm with his brother-in-law Robert Pearsall, Elizabeth's husband, in the selling of dry goods. It seems probable that Isaac was already thinking about his retirement.

The printing shop issued seventy imprints from 1801 through 1805, most of them on religious topics. Six were works by the English Baptist theologian Andrew Fuller, whose writings reflect the struggle against what he and others of similar persuasion considered a relaxation of moral obligation. Beilby Porteus, the bishop of London, wrote a *Summary of the Principal Evidences for the Truth and Divine Origin of the Christian Revelation,* which Collins issued twice in 1800. Another work was by Henry Scougal, the Scottish divine, whose *Life of God in the Soul of Man* the printer issued in 1802. Porteus's chief aim was to enforce the observance of religious holidays, and he, like Fuller, accused Thomas Paine of being an adversary of the Gospel. His *Age of Reason,* Porteus held, rendered "irreligion easy to the meanest capacity." [24]

Collins's own views often coincided with those of his authors. Bishop Porteus conducted a private war against Sunday concerts, and Collins, whose piety seems to have increased over the years, insisted: "Plays and Playhouses have been the Bane and Ruin of Thousands, as they sow the Seeds of every species of Vice and Immorality. I hope I have not a child that would be seen at one of them—it would disgrace them in the Eyes of all good Men." [25]

Collins's staple items were those by Lindley Murray. Of the shop's fifteen imprints of 1802, for example, five were books by Murray. Collins continued also to publish Fénelon's works.

New York booksellers and printers in 1802 turned their attention to an event the *Daily Advertiser* heralded as the "first Literary Fair ever held in the United States." It was the result of a proposal by Mathew Carey, the famous Philadelphia printer, that there should be instituted in this country regular literary fairs similar to those held in Germany. Carey was named secretary of the first one, and Collins's friend and Pearl Street neighbor Hugh Gaine was appointed chairman in recognition of his long service to America's young printing industry. On the last day of May a large number of booksellers from the eastern states, as well as from Philadelphia and Baltimore, arrived in New York, having sent ahead samples of their work to be exhibited, sold, or exchanged.

The fair was held at the Old Coffee House from June 1 to June 7. In addition to Gaine and Collins, the New York book trade was represented by Thomas and James Swords, Thomas B. Jansen, David Longworth, Evert Duyckinck, William Falconer, G. F. Hopkins, Samuel Campbell, E. M. Boyle, T. S. Arden, Peter A. Mesier, William Durell, James Oram, and Napthali Judah. Most of the New York delegation had shops along Pearl Street. From Philadelphia, in addition to Carey, came Samuel F. Bradford, William Duane, Patrick Bryne, William Y. Buch, Abraham Small, and Jacob Johnson. Also in attendance were men from New Haven, Albany, Richmond, and the state of New Hampshire.

On the final day the booksellers were urged "to improve the quality of the books they publish" and "to discontinue the importation of all books, of which good and correct editions are printed in this country." [26] The group resolved to hold another fair in Philadelphia the next October and to sponsor two each year thereafter, in New York each April and in Philadelphia each October. In 1804 the Collins firm won a silver medal for a specimen of printing shown at the Philadelphia fair.

In the spring of 1805, when Benjamin Perkins became a full partner, the company announced a general expansion of its business. If the senior partner was about to retire, the company he had founded was embarking on a new period of growth, for it advertised as follows:

BOOK-SELLING

In this department they have the satisfaction of announcing, that they are now opening, in addition to their former stock, an extensive assortment of very valuable Books, recently imported from London, where they were selected with great care, and bound with peculiar neatness for a private library—The collection in the different branches of science and literature, especially in Medicine, Botany, Chemistry, Agriculture, Electricity, Belles-Lettres, and the Greek and Latin Classics, is particularly valuable. Having formed connections which will enable them to procure on the most favorable terms all English publications of merit, the public may depend on their exertions to keep their store constantly supplied.

PRINTING

This branch, also, they propose carrying on more extensively. One of the first works of magnitude which they are preparing to execute, is a *new edition* of the *Quarto Family Bible,* generally know [sic] by the name of "Collins' Bible," originally printed and published by Isaac Collins. The new edition is intended to be a *fac simile* of the former one, with the exception that it will be printed with a handsomer type, and on a white paper.

STATIONERY

Account Books of every variety and paper, and indeed all articles usually classed under this head will be kept constantly on hand.

Arrangements are making for associating the *Bookbinding Business* with the above branches.[27]

This notice appeared in the *Spectator* throughout May and June, and on June 5 "Collins, Perkins & Co." reported that it had just published Murray's *English Grammar,* an impression, "which, it is believed, is the only one in the United States . . . printed from the ninth English edition." Throughout August, September, and October the company printed proposals for republishing by subscription the Collins quarto Bible. As in 1791, subscribers could order Ostervald's *Notes* and the Apocrypha separately. The base price was set at $5.50 for the Bible bound in sheep and lettered. For fifty cents more the purchaser could have the Apocrypha bound with the Bible. The *Notes* alone added a dollar to the base price, and for a total of $7.50 the purchaser received both the Apocrypha and the *Notes* bound with the Bible. An extra fifty cents was charged in all cases for binding in calf.

In November and December 1805 Collins and Perkins advertised "Elegant Writing Papers," pencils, inkpowders, sealing wax, pounce, and pounce boxes. Area businessmen could look to this "new" company for "every article used in the Counting House." The firm continued this newspaper promotion, listing, among numerous items, William Mavor's twenty-five-volume *Universal History,* Henry Tuke's Quaker classic, *Principles of Religion,* and two inexpensive schoolbooks by Murray, his *English Spelling Book* and his *First Book for Children.* The speller sold for $2 a dozen and the primer for seventy-five cents. In February 1806, nearly a year after the formation of the new partnership, the notices often ran as long as one and a half columns in the *Spectator.* Listed were as many as 135 titles, including a "superb edition" of David Hume's *History of Great Britain,* described as "one of the most elegant works ever executed." And at an elegant price, too, for the set of six volumes imported from England sold for $450.

Another Collins firm began advertising in the same

newspaper in March 1806, first announcing the partnership of Charles Collins and Robert Pearsall and then
noting their stock of broadcloths, flannels, and linens.
Their store was located at 268 Pearl Street, but the business hardly managed to survive its first year. Isaac Collins
reported that his son had failed in the endeavor, losing
a "full thirty thousand dollars by bad Debts." [28]

Although the eldest of Isaac's sons failed to acquire
the father's Quaker sense of business, Charles became
almost fanatical about some elements of Quaker liberalism. So impenetrable and unalterable were Charles's con-
victions on the evils of slavery that the story is told of his
once refusing to share another Quaker's umbrella because
it was made of cotton. As a follower of Isaac T. Hopper,
founder of the Anti-Slavery Society, he also insisted that
the books he purchased not be tied with string made
from southern cotton. He was said to have resigned his
membership in a meeting house in protest over the lack of
a stern antislavery attitude among the congregation. In
1808 Charles helped incorporate the New York Manu-
mission Society, a group whose founders had included
Alexander Hamilton, Robert Bowne, John Jay, John
Murray, and John Murray, Jr.

Collins's announcement of his retirement and the company's announcement that it had nearly completed the
printing of the Bible both appeared in May 1806. In the
"Dissolution of Copartnership," dated May 1, Collins
agreed to relinquish his share and interest in the business.
For their part, Perkins and Thomas Collins agreed to pay
Isaac $8,000, one-third of the company's estimated
worth. They agreed to keep the name Collins, Perkins &

Co. for one year, after which it was to be changed to Collins and Perkins. Isaac, in turn, agreed to help complete the printing of the Bible, a service for which Perkins and young Collins paid him $1,000. This indebtedness was explicit: ". . . the reputation of which Edition will very much depend on the known attention and superintendance of the said Isaac Collins and his family, and the future profits of which when published, it is probable will be considerable." The fee was not to be paid until a year after the Bible was published.[29]

Collins made plans to retire almost immediately after his wife's death. On January 28, 1806, George Dillwyn, living in Burlington, wrote the printer in anticipation of his leave-taking: "I note thy prospect of retiring from business; and if thy partiality for Jersey should prove a means of thy being readded to our little company here, before we are detached from it, I believe it will be a pleasing circumstance to all." [30]

Collins sat for the artist John Wesley Jarvis at his Nassau Street studio on several occasions in 1806. Jarvis, who had acquired a reputation as an engraver, turned to portrait work in 1803 or 1804, although, according to his biographer, it was not until 1808 that he mastered the new form.[31] Collins was among the artist's first subjects. The pose is undramatic, as in most of Jarvis's early portraits. Collins's face and shoulders are turned slightly to the right, and the printer appears tense and stony-faced. There is hardly the hint of a smile, and the colors, now darkened by age, are somber; one is left with the impression of a man of few words and little patience. Collins was sixty when the portrait was painted.

One of Collins's several grandchildren, a daughter of Susannah Collins Smith, describes him this way:

> He certainly was a stern, not to say a severe, man in his family, and yet with his strong sense of duty he was very desirous of providing educational advantages for them and giving his sons a good start in business. His social position was of the best; an excellent provider, his table was always well supplied. Our Aunt Rebecca Grellet was his favorite child, and when the young Etienne, the French refugee, had the temerity to ask him for her hand, the favor was most unwillingly granted, and only after much conflict and much consideration.
>
> Grandfather was very neat and tasty in his dress. His fine Holland linen and his peach-blossom vests and short clothes with white silk or thread stockings were the admiration of his daughters; and when he made an evening call, the good-wives of his acquaintance were wont to say, "Here comes Mr. Collins. We know him by his carefulness in scraping and wiping his shoes upon the mat as he enters." [32]

Collins shifted his attention from the business world of the city to a "quiet Habitation" in the country. "My great —my sore Bereavement is still very heavy with me," he wrote to his nephew Archibald Bartram in November 1806, "and when it will feel less so, I do not know." He continued: "We are getting forward with the Bible, being almost through first Chronicles and now have two Presses running pretty steadily on it. But Business to me is no longer any pleasure, nor have I much inducement to continue at it longer than will be sufficient to complete this work. I have pretty much made up my mind to retire into the country to a quiet Habitation and there mourn out the remainder of my days which may not be many." [33]

On January 10, 1807, the dissolution of the company became final, as reported on that date in the press. In the same public notice the new company of Collins and Perkins reported: "Their edition, just completed of the Quarto Family Bible, embellished with elegant engravings, and their editions of Lindley Murray's popular SCHOOL BOOKS, carefully printed from the latest English copies . . . Their assortment in Medicine, Surgery and Anatomy, Chemistry, Electricity, and General Science, which is already not inferior to any in the city, will be constantly enlarging; and Physicians and others may depend on being supplied on the most favorable terms." [34]

In the preface to this second edition of his Bible, the Old Testament of which bears the imprint date of 1806, Collins stated that a "great price" was paid for the engravings, procured from the "first artists of our country, and some from an eminent engraver lately from London." He said that the firm held a competition, awarding a gold medal to the artists who produced the best plates, which Collins regarded as specimens "of the degree of perfection to which the art of line engraving has advanced in the United States." Subscribers could order the Bible with or without engravings, just as they could with the Apocrypha and Ostervald's *Notes*.

In a short period of time the firm which Collins had nurtured through many stages in Burlington, then Trenton, and finally New York, had become one of the country's leading scientific publishing houses. The Collins and Perkins firm, by 1807 official printer to the New York Hospital and importer of medical books for its library, listed as many as one hundred medical titles alone, not all of which, however, were its own imprints.

A vital part of the business continued to depend on the subscription books and, consequently, the firm solicited the patronage of prominent American experts. Dr. Benjamin Rush, the famous Philadelphia physician, was one of several such persons called upon by Collins and Perkins. In December 1808, for instance, Isaac Collins, Jr., who had since joined the company, wrote Dr. Rush for his endorsement of two books on anatomy and surgery that the company planned to publish. Young Collins asked for the doctor's signature at the head of the subscription lists that would include "several of the most eminent physicians of our country." [35]

Another time the company asked Dr. Rush to help revise an English volume so that it would be more applicable to the "peculiar diseases of this country." "We especially allude to his [the author's] ideas of the Yellow Fever, of its contagion, and of the plan of treatment." Collins and Perkins wanted Rush to write either marginal notes or an appendix. Rush declined the offer and advised them to consult Dr. Edward Miller, the New York physician who, along with Dr. Valentine Seaman and others, was a leader in combating yellow fever. Evidence of the publishers' strong interest in public health was their fear that "if we do not immediately put the work to press with . . . improvements, some other bookseller will undertake it and probably without any alterations or additions in which case the work may tend to promote a material and egregious error." [36]

Isaac Collins, his Bible and business in younger but trusted hands, returned to Burlington in early 1808, where, as Isaiah Thomas put it, "he was enabled to retire and enjoy, in the society of his friends, the rewards of his industry." [37] As Collins himself had prophesied, his life was to end where his industry had begun. From a letter to his daughter Sarah one detects a change of spirit in the bereaved widower and the retired printer of earlier correspondence:

> I am pleased with the premises I occupy, My Peas are in Blossom, Carrots, Beets and Parsnips are up—Sallad of divers kind on the Table when we please. Potatoes are also up, and I have planted various kinds of Pole, Dwarf and Lima Beans, and I have gotten some Cabbage plants set out. We have a very great show of Strawberries, Raspberries, Currants, Plums, and some Gooseberries, several small Cherry trees full of fruit. We have been too much engaged about many Things: There is so much to do that by Night every day we go to bed weary—sleep some—rise betimes and at it again.[38]

Collins purchased a house of his own at York and Broad Streets in July 1808. In 1808 also he met Mrs. Deborah Smith, a widow with two children about the ages of Stacy and Joseph Collins, who had accompanied their father from New York to Burlington. Isaac and Deborah were married on October 9, 1809, and they passed the next eight years in leisure, entertaining Isaac's children and grandchildren, who often visited Burlington, and traveling short distances to visit friends and relatives.

"This would be a delightful place for Stephen & Rebecca, if they could feel it so," Isaac wrote Sarah, soon after his move. "She would improve in her Health— there being plenty of Physicians for Soul & Body. Thee & Susan I believe must take turn about in keeping house for the Boys so that each of you may partake of the sweets of the delightful Spot. I shall long to see all my Children & Grandchildren here by turns and their passing back & forward will contribute to their health." [39]

In 1811 Isaac's youngest child, Joseph, left Burlington to return to New York, the last of the family to enter the printing business now managed by his brothers. "The Business is that of *his choice*," Isaac informed Susannah, "and I hope after a while he will become quite reconciled to the disagreeable part of it." Thomas, who had followed Charles in the printing trade, but with more success, had in turn been followed by William, Benjamin, Isaac, Jr., Stacy, and now Joseph. They all remained, however, within reach of their father's influence and financial aid. Their sister Anna, who never married, seems to have been both her father's representative and her brothers' refuge in New York.

Sometime in 1816—the exact date is not known—Collins became ill and for several months suffered from what was described as a "painful malady which often deprived him of social intercourse and put his fortitude to the severest test." [40] He died of a stroke on March 21, 1817, in his seventy-second year, and was buried in the Quaker cemetery near the site of the old meeting house where he had worshiped from 1770 to 1777 (this had since been torn down and a new one built in its place). Collins's estate was inventoried at nearly $36,000, and his will stipulated "all houses and lands to be sold," but his wife to receive most of the household goods. Deborah also received her husband's shares in a Philadelphia bank and the Burlington Aqueduct Company. Isaac's sister Elizabeth was to receive the interest on $500 for the rest of her life, "at her death the principal to be divided between children of my half-sister Sarah McQuire." [41]

To his seven sons went Collins's books, and in addition Isaac, Jr., received his silver watch and Joseph, a case of razors. To his six daughters went the family silver, except what belonged to Deborah at their marriage. He bequeathed $3,000 to each child—except Charles, "having had his share but having been unsuccessful in trade," and William, "having had his share," who received $1,000 each. Thomas had received his share earlier as a partner in the printing company. However, he was awarded a Spanish milled dollar. Isaac, Jr. and Stephen Grellet were executors of the estate.

The Collins publishing house, the substantial part of Isaac's legacy, secure in the hands of another generation, continued to flourish in New York for many years after its founder's death. In 1810, following the death of Benjamin Perkins, the name had been changed to Collins & Co., with Thomas at the head. He and his younger brothers carried on the business at the old address until 1822, at which time Joseph, the youngest, who earlier had gone into a brief stereotyping partnership with Benjamin, opened a printing shop at 117 Maiden Lane.[42] Benjamin, meanwhile, had opened a bookstore at 230 Pearl Street with Samuel Hannay. He withdrew from the firm in 1832, the business being continued by Hannay and George B. Collins, the only son of Charles Collins. Benjamin and Stacy got back together in 1835 under the name of B. & S. Collins, replacing Collins & Hannay. In 1838, with John Keese having joined them, the firm of Collins, Keese & Co. moved to 254 Pearl, where the printing and publishing business that Isaac Collins had founded was continued for nearly thirty more years by his sons and grandsons.[43]

❧

The life of Isaac Collins illustrates many things about eighteenth-century American printing. Craftsmen like Collins lived and worked during a pioneering period, what Franklin called the "age of experiments." They were men of destiny in that everything they achieved, every innovation, however small, was to have a lasting influence. Collins, who contributed to the age in no small way, was an individualist and an astute businessman at a time when nearly as many printers failed as succeeded in business.

Although townspeople knew Collins as an active Quaker, the proud head of a large family, they thought of him first, and with affection, as "Mr. Collins, Printer." Printers were among the most respected members of their towns. Collins ranked high in this regard, as many personal and professional friends, including authors, affirmed. Not only were printers respected because of the "power of the press"; they were respected because they were interesting and knowledgeable people, if occasionally a bit eccentric.

Their shops were popular centers of congregation, where townspeople went to buy dry goods, patent medicines, and notions, as well as to acquire the latest books and pamphlets by foreign and American writers. If, as in Collins's case during most of the Revolution, the local printer issued a weekly newspaper, townspeople could also get the latest news and discuss the issues of the day, among themselves or with Mr. Collins.

Early printers were comparatively well-to-do, though financial success in those days depended as much on ability to withstand the uncertainties of the business as it did on professional skill. If one held the important post of government printer, as Collins did for a quarter of a century in New Jersey, he was often able to amass a sizable fortune. Toward the end of his career Collins owned two houses, one adjacent to his New York City shop and store and the other some distance away in the country. Upon his retirement in 1808, at which time he was paid $8,000, or one-third of the estimated worth of the Collins firm, he purchased a $4,000 house in Burlington, New Jersey. When he died, his estate was valued at nearly $36,000.

Collins was more affluent than most of his fellows, though perhaps more frugal by nature. The mere fact that he conducted his business for nearly forty years, without interruption, is evidence of his material success. When he moved from Philadelphia to Burlington and then on to Trenton and New York, he did so because of the new challenges each town presented and not because of any failure to cope with the old. The firm that he left continued to flourish for another sixty-seven years, an honored and increasingly profitable business.

No printer who published a newspaper in Collins's time became rich on that enterprise alone. In fact, the wealthy ones, like Isaiah Thomas, and the poor ones, like William Goddard, were wealthy or poor according to whether they devoted themselves to the publication and sale of books or to the somewhat less profitable newspaper business. Collins liked both, and it is to his credit that he sacrificed money and security during the years he edited and printed the *New-Jersey Gazette*. He started the *Gazette* with the help of legislative support and money, but when the money ran out, instead of discontinuing the paper, he carried it on against great odds for nearly nine years.

It was during this period, however, that Collins probably exerted his greatest influence; and it is the character of his newspaper no less than the quality of his books that assures him lasting renown. The meticulously edited and printed pages of the *Gazette* constitute an enduring source of information and pleasure. It was one of the best-looking papers of the time, and its editor was one of the staunchest defenders of freedom of the press in an era when even the thought of publishing a paper was risky business. He saw himself as "a faithful guardian of the Liberty of the Press" and resisted several attempts to censor the *Gazette*. Editions of the paper were liked or disliked, usually depending on which side of the issues editor and readers happened to be from week to week. Yet Collins persisted in his pride and his purse.

Collins's decision to delay his retirement long enough to see through the printing of the second edition of his famous quarto Bible also says a lot in terms of the man. The first edition, printed in Trenton in 1791, marked the high point in his professional life; with the completion of the 1807 edition in New York City he ended a career of nearly fifty years in the printing trade. His Bible is the best example of his craftsmanship, for it is without significant error and is bound in the finest leathers and tooled in good taste. There is no mistaking the quality of any of his more than two hundred and fifty separate imprints.

To the regret of the biographer, the full measure of Collins's character and achievements will almost certainly never be known, for of the few letters and papers that he left, most are concerned with the routine of his business as a master printer. Still, Collins emerges clearly as a man of exemplary qualities, a man who would not willingly compromise on matters of truth or principle or the high professional standards he set himself. The numerous references to him in the minutes of Quaker meetings and his years of service to the Trenton Academy, one of the country's early nondenominational "public" schools, are indicative of his religious and civic concerns. Moreover, he enjoyed long and warm acquaintance with some of the social, political, economic, and religious leaders of his time.

One of Collins's grandchildren, Maria S. Reeve, writing many years after his death, recalled that he was a little above medium height, somewhat taller than any of his sons, dignified and rather reserved in manner. "I remember him as one to be somewhat feared, perhaps as the same time warmly loved, and I thought it a great privilege to be allowed to wait upon him." [44]

A LIST OF
COLLINS
IMPRINTS

This list includes all of the known imprints issued by Isaac Collins in Philadelphia, Burlington, Trenton, and New York City. Many titles have been abbreviated and modernized in my text, but detailed information, including imprint size and repository identification, is available in the following checklists: Charles R. Hildeburn, *A Century of Printing: The Issues of the Press in Pennsylvania, 1685–1784* (Philadelphia, 1885–1886) ; William Nelson, *Check-List of the Issues of the Press of New Jersey, 1723, 1728, 1754–1800* (Paterson, N.J., 1899) ; Constance H. Humphrey, "Check-List of New Jersey Imprints to the End of the Revolution," *Papers of the Bibliographical Society of America,* Vol. 24 (1930), pp. 43–149; Lucille M. Morsch, "A Checklist of New Jersey Imprints, 1784–1800," *WPA Historical Records Survey Project* (1939) ; and Charles F. Heartman, *Preliminary Checklist of Almanacs Printed in New Jersey Prior to 1850* (New York, 1929).

The following larger bibliographies also list New Jersey imprints: Charles Evans, *American Bibliography, 1639–1799,* 12 vols. (Chicago, 1903–1934), which Clifford K. Shipton brought through 1800 in a thirteenth volume published in 1955 and to which Roger P. Bristol added an author-title index in 1959 and an index of printers in 1961; Ralph R. Shaw and Richard H. Shoemaker, *American Bibliography: A Preliminary Checklist,* which picks up where Shipton left off and continues through 1820 with separate volumes for each year; and Clarence S. Brigham, *History and Bibliography of American Newspapers, 1690–1820,* 2 vols. (Worcester, Mass., 1947).

Though the present list is based essentially on the above works, I have added information that I collected during my explorations for Collins imprints in the old book collections of libraries in New Jersey, Pennsylvania, and New York. Although the purpose of my search was not so much to examine Collins titles for bibliographical detail as it was to increase my knowledge of the printing craft during the eighteenth century, I hope that the list—a composite of the work of several persons—will prove useful.

NEWSPAPERS
AND ALMANACS

Burlington Almanack (Burlington), 1770–1777
New-Jersey Gazette (Burlington), Dec. 5, 1777–Feb. 25, 1778
New-Jersey Gazette (Trenton), March 4, 1778–Nov. 27, 1786
New-Jersey Almanack (Trenton), 1778–1795

BOOKS AND
PAMPHLETS

Cluny, Alexander, *The American Traveller*. Philadelphia: Crukshank and Collins. 1770. 89 pp.

Davies, Richard, *An Account of the Convincement, Exercises, Services and Travels of . . . Richard Davies*. 3rd Edition. Philadelphia: Crukshank and Collins, 1770, 286 pp.

Edwards, Rev. Morgan, *Materials Towards a History of the American Baptists*, Vol. I. Philadelphia: Crukshank and Collins. 1770. 138 pp.

Gessner, Solomon, *The Death of Abel*. Philadelphia: Crukshank and Collins. 1770. 106 pp.

Kearsley, Dr. John, Jr., *A Narrative of Many Facts, Relating to the Late Disputed Will of Samuel Flower*. Philadelphia: Crukshank and Collins. 1770. 16 pp.

Milton, John, *An Old Looking-Glass for the Laity and Clergy of All Denominations, Who Either Give or Receive Money Under Pretence of the Gospel . . . Considerations Touching the Likeliest Means to Remove Hirelings Out of the Church of Christ*. Philadelphia: Crukshank and Collins. 1770. 74 pp.

Sauvages, François Bossier de, and Samuel Pullien, *Directions for the Breeding and Management of Silk-Worms*. Philadelphia: Crukshank and Collins. 1770. 32 pp.

Marmontel, Jean François, *The History of Belisarius, the Heroik and Humane Roman General*. Burlington: Isaac Collins. 1770. 135 pp.

Chandler, Rev. Thomas Bradbury, *A Sermon Preached Before the Corporation for the Relief of the Widows and Children of Clergymen, in the Communion of the Church of England in America.* Burlington: Isaac Collins. 1771. 76 pp.

Moody, Thomas [pseud.], *A Compendium of Surveying; or the Surveyor's Pocket Companion.* Burlington: Isaac Collins. 1771. 48 pp.

Dodsley, Robert, *The Oeconomy of Human Life.* [Translated from an Indian manuscript, written by an ancient Brahmin, and includes an account of the manner in which the manuscript was discovered.] Two Parts. Burlington: Isaac Collins. 1771. 54, 70 pp.

Woolman, John, *An Epistle to the Quarterly and Monthly Meetings of Friends.* Burlington: Isaac Collins. 1772. 16 pp.

Benezet, Anthony, *Brief Considerations on Slavery, and the Expediency of its Abolition.* Burlington: Isaac Collins. 1773. 16 pp.

Christ, the Christian's Life: In a Sermon on John XIV, 19. Burlington: Isaac Collins. 1773. 29 pp.

Mason, William, *Methodism Displayed.* 6th edition enlarged. Burlington: Isaac Collins. 1773. 31 pp.

Relly, Rev. James, *A Short Specimen of Apostolick Preaching.* Burlington, N.J. 1773.

Sharp, Granville, *An Essay on Slavery, Proving from Scripture Its Inconsistency with Humanity and Religion.* [Includes opinions of other writers on slavery.] Burlington: Isaac Collins. 1773. 28 pp.

Baxter, Richard, *The Saints Everlasting Rest.* [A Christian Library, Vol. 37.] Burlington: Isaac Collins. 1774. 442 pp.

Jones, David, *A Journal of Two Visits Made to Some Nations of Indians on the West Side of the River Ohio, in the Years 1772 and 1773.* Burlington: Isaac Collins. 1774. 95 pp.

Sewel, William, *The History of the Rise, Increase and Progress of the Christian People Called Quakers.* 3rd Edition. Burlington: Isaac Collins. 1774. 828 pp.

Crowley, Ann, *Some Expressions of Ann Crowley, Daughter of Thomas and Mary Crowley, of London, During Her Last Illness.* 3rd Edition. Ed. Thomas Crowley. Burlington: Isaac Collins. 1775. 30 pp.

Fisher, George [pseud.], *The Instructor: or, Young Man's Companion.* 21st Edition Corrected and Improved. Burlington: Isaac Collins. 1775. 372 pp.

Relly, James and John, *Christian Hymns, Poems, and Spiritual Songs, Sacred to the Praise of God our Saviour.* Burlington: Isaac Collins. 1776. 247 pp.

Benezet, Anthony, *The Mighty Destroyer Displayed, in Some Account of the Dreadful Havock Made by the Mistaken Use as well as Abuse of Distilled Spirituous Liquors.* Trenton: Isaac Collins. 1779. 48 pp.

New Testament. Trenton: Isaac Collins. 1779. 348 pp. [The pages from 325 to the end are misnumbered 345–368.]

The New England Primer, Improved. Trenton: Isaac Collins. 1780.

New Testament. Trenton: Isaac Collins. 1780.

Smith, Samuel Stanhope, *A Funeral Sermon on the Death of the Hon. Richard Stockton.* Trenton: Isaac Collins. 1781. 48 pp.

New Testament. Trenton: Isaac Collins. 1782. 348 pp. [Appears to be a reprint of the 1779 New Testament with pagination corrected.]

Livingston, William, *Philosophic Solitude: or, the Choice of a Rural Life: Poem.* Trenton: Isaac Collins. 1782. 28 pp.

Paine, Thomas, *Letter Addressed to the Abbé Raynal on the Affairs of North America.* Trenton. Isaac Collins. 1782. 70 pp.

Benezet, Anthony, *A Serious Address to the Rulers of America, on the Inconsistency of their Conduct Respecting Slavery.* Trenton: Isaac Collins. 1783. 22 pp.

Collins, Isaac, *Proposals . . . for Printing a New Edition of the Journals of Congress.* Trenton. 1785. 3 pp.

Price, Richard, *Observations on the Importance of the American Revolution, and the Means of Making It a Benefit to the World.* Trenton: Isaac Collins. 1785. 88 pp.

Ramsay, David, *The History of the Revolution of South-Carolina, from a British Province to an Independent State.* 2 vols. Trenton: Isaac Collins. 1785. 453, 574 pp.

Dilworth, Thomas, *A New Guide to the English Tongue, in Five Parts* Trenton: Isaac Collins. 1786.

Proceedings of the Convention of the Protestant Episcopal Church, in the State of New-Jersey. Trenton: Isaac Collins. 1787. 42 pp.

Symmes, John Cleves, *To the Respectable Public.* Trenton: Isaac Collins. 1787. 30 pp.

New Testament. Trenton: Isaac Collins. 1788. 232 unpaged leaves.

New Testament. Trenton: Isaac Collins. 1788. 359 pp.

Minto, Walter, *An Inaugural Oration on the Progress and Importance of the Mathematical.* Trenton: Isaac Collins. 1788. 51 pp.

Proceedings of the 5th Convention of the Protestant Episcopal Church in New-Jersey. Trenton: Isaac Collins. 1788. Pp. 44–48.

Catalogus Collegii Naeo-Caesariensis. Trenton: Isaaci Collins. 1789. 16 pp.

Collins, Isaac, *Proposals for Printing by Subscription . . . the Holy Bible.* Trenton. 1789. 4 pp.

Proceedings of the 6th Convention of the Protestant Episcopal Church in New-Jersey. Trenton: Isaac Collins. 1789. Pp. 50–57.

Downame, John, *A Brief Concordance or Table to the Bible.* [Issued with Collins's Bible of 1791.] Trenton: Isaac Collins. 1790. 72 pp.

Proceedings of a Convention of the Protestant Episcopal Church in New-Jersey. Trenton: Isaac Collins. 1790. 22 pp.

Woodhull, John, *A Sermon, for the Day of Publick Thanksgiving.* Trenton: Isaac Collins. 1790. 24 pp.

Hart, Oliver, *A Gospel Church Portrayed, and Her Orderly Service Pointed Out: A Sermon.* Trenton: Isaac Collins. 1791. 38 pp.

The Holy Bible. Trenton: Isaac Collins. 1791. 1160 pp.

Ostervald, Jean Frederic, *Practical Observations on the Old and New Testaments.* [Issued with Collins's Bible of 1791.] Trenton: Isaac Collins. 1791. 156 pp.

Catalogus Collegii Naeo-Caesariensis. Trenton: Isaaci Collins. 1792. 16 pp.

The Holy Bible. [O.T. 1793, N.T. 1794.] Trenton: Isaac Collins. 1118 pp.

Minutes of the Philadelphia Baptist Association (Southampton, Bucks County, Pa., Oct. 29–30, 1793). Trenton: Isaac Collins. 1793. 7 pp.

Phipps, Joseph, *The Original and Present State of Man, Briefly Considered.* Trenton: Isaac Collins. 1793. 228 pp.

Catalogus Collegii Naeo-Caesariensis. Trenton: Isaaci Collins. 1794. 15 pp.

Laws of the College of New-Jersey. Trenton: Isaac Collins. 1794. 15 pp.

New Testament. [Bound with the Old Testament, 1793.] Trenton: Isaac Collins. 1794. 260 pp.

Grubb, Sarah (Tuke), *Some Account of the Life and Religious Labours of Sarah Grubb.* Trenton: Isaac Collins. 1795. 418 pp.

Murray, Lindley, *The Power of Religion on the Mind.* 7th Edition, Corrected and Enlarged. Trenton: Isaac Collins. 1795. 220 pp.

Dell, William, *The Doctrine of Baptism.* 11th Edition. New York: Isaac Collins. 1796. 28 pp.

Savery, William, *Three Sermons Preached at the Meeting-House of the People Commonly Called Quakers.* [First two by Savery and third by George Dillwyn.] 3rd Edition. New York: Isaac Collins. 1797. 55 pp.

Scott, Job, *Journal of the Life, Travels and Gospel Labours of that Faithful Servant and Minister of Christ, Job Scott.* New York: Isaac Collins. 1797. 360 pp.

Scott, Job, *Journal,* etc. 4th Edition. New York: Isaac Collins. 1798. 360 pp.

Barruel, Augustin de, The Abbé, *Memoirs, Illustrating the History of Jacobinism.* Part III, Vol. III, *The Antisocial Conspiracy.* New York: Isaac Collins. 1799. 256 pp.

Fénelon, François de Salignac de la Mothe, Archevêque de Cambray, *Some Advice to Governesses and Teachers.* New York: Isaac Collins. 1799. 12 pp.

Livingston, John Henry, *Two Sermons, Delivered before the New-York Missionary Society.* [First by Rev. Dr. Livingston and the second by Rev. Dr. John M'Knight.] New York: Isaac Collins. 1799. 104 pp.

Murray, Lindley, *The English Reader; or, Pieces in Prose and Poetry, Selected from the Best Writers.* New York: Isaac Collins. 1799. 359 pp.

Fox, George, *A Journal, or Historical Account, of the Life, Travels, Sufferings of George Fox.* 4th Edition. 2 vols. New York: Isaac Collins. 1800. 440, 464 pp.

Hutchinson, William, *The Spirit of Masonry*. New York: Isaac Collins. 1800. 196 pp.

Linn, William, *A Discourse, Delivered April 1st, 1800, in the Brick Presbyterian Church, Before the New-York Missionary Society*. New York: Isaac Collins. 1800. 20 pp.

——, *A Funeral Eulogy, Occasioned by the Death of General Washington*. New York: Isaac Collins. 1800. 44 pp.

Murray, Lindley, *English Grammar*. 3rd Edition. New York: Isaac Collins. 1800. 248 pp.

——, *The English Reader*, etc. 2nd Edition. New York: Isaac Collins. 1800. 366 pp.

Rules of Discipline, and Christian Advices, of the Yearly Meeting of Friends for the State of New-York and Parts Adjacent. New York: Isaac Collins. 1800. 141 pp.

Seaman, Valentine, *The Midwives Monitor, and Mothers Mirror*. New York: Isaac Collins. 1800. 123 pp.

Abeel, John Nelson, *A Discourse, Delivered April 6th, 1801 . . . Before the New-York Missionary Society*. New York: Isaac Collins. 1801. 67 pp.

Brayton, Mrs. Patience Greene, *Extracts . . . from the Life and Religious Labours of Patience Brayton*. New York: Collins and Son. 1801. 5 pp.

——, *A Short Account of the Life and Religious Labours of Patience Brayton*. New York: Collins and Son. 1801. 135 pp.

Coleman, William, *Cases of Practice, Adjudged in the Supreme Court of the State of New-York*. New York: Isaac Collins. 1801. 152 pp.

Eddy, Thomas, *An Account of the State Prison, or Penitentiary House, in the City of New-York*. New York: Collins and Son. 1801. 97 pp.

Fénelon, François de Salignac de la Mothe, *On Faithfulness in Little Things*. New York: Isaac Collins. 1801.

Fuller, Andrew, *The Gospel Its Own Witness*. New York: Isaac Collins. 1801. 275 pp.

——, *The Gospel Worthy of All Acceptation*. 3rd Edition. New York: Isaac Collins and Son. 1801. 222 pp.

——, *A Summary of the Principal Evidences for the Truth, and Divine Origin, of the Christian Revelation*. New York: Isaac Collins. 1801. 72 pp.

Immens, Peter, *The Pious Communicant*. New York: Isaac Collins and Son. 1801. 248 pp.

Lessons for Youth. New York: Isaac Collins and Son. 1801.

Murray, Lindley, *Sequel to the English Reader*, etc. New York: Isaac Collins. 1801. 376 pp.

Porteus, Beilby, *A Summary of the Principal Evidences for the Truth and Divine Origin of the Christian Revelation*. 3rd Edition. New York: Isaac Collins. 1801. 72 pp.

Caines, George, *An Enquiry into the Law Merchant of the United States,* Vol. I. New York: Isaac Collins and Son. 1802.

Constitution for the Government of the New-York Institute for the Inoculation of the Kine Pock. New York: Collins and Son. 1802. 11 pp.

Facts and Observations Relative to the Kine-Pock. New York: Collins and Son. 1802. 28 pp.

Fuller, Andrew, *The Backslider.* New York: Isaac Collins and Son. 1802. 99 pp.

——, *The Christian Doctrine of Rewards.* [Bound with *The Backslider.*] New York: Isaac Collins and Son. 1892. 36 pp.

——, *God's Approbation.* [Bound with *The Backslider.*] New York: Isaac Collins and Son. 1802. 51 pp.

Jeffrys, John, *Some Passages of the Life of John Jeffrys.* New York: Isaac Collins and Son. 1802. 46 pp.

Mason, John Mitchell, *Living Faith.* New York: Isaac Collins and Son. 1802. 35 pp.

Murray, Lindley, *An Abridgement of . . . English Grammar.* 6th Edition. New York: Isaac Collins and Son. 1802.

——, *English Grammar.* 6th Edition. New York: Isaac Collins and Son. 1802. 274 pp.

——, *The English Reader,* etc. New York: Isaac Collins and Son. 1802. 366 pp.

——, *Introduction to the English Reader.* New York: Isaac Collins and Son. 1802. 218 pp.

——, *The Power of Religion on the Mind.* 10th Edition. New York: Isaac Collins and Son. 1802. 280 pp.

Rawes, William, Jr., *Examples for Youth.* New York: Isaac Collins and Son. 1802. 263 pp.

Scougal, Henry, *The Life of God in the Soul of Man.* New York: Isaac Collins and Son. 1802. 113 pp.

The American Orthographer; or, New Book of Spelling. 2 pts. New York: Isaac Collins and Son. 1803.

Caritat, Henry, *A Catalogue of the Library of H. Caritat's Literary Room, New-York.* New York: Isaac Collins and Son. 1803. 36 pp.

Fénelon, François de Salignac de la Mothe, *Pious Reflections.* New York: Isaac Collins and Son. 1803. 114 pp.

Mavor, William Fordyce, *A Preliminary View of Universal History; Together with a History of the Antediluvians of Ancient Egypt, and the Neighbouring Nations.* New York: Isaac Collins and Son. 1803. 345 pp.

Missionary Society of Connecticut, *Interesting Account of Religion in France.* New York: Isaac Collins and Son. 1803.

Murray, Lindley, *English Exercises.* 7th Edition. New York: Isaac Collins and Son. 1803. 204 pp.

Murray, Lindley, *A Key to the Exercises,* etc. New-York: Isaac Collins and Son. 1803. 156 pp.

——, *Lecteur Français: ou, Recueil de pièces, en prose et en vers.* New York: Collins père et fils. 1803. 403 pp.

Society of Friends, *To the Citizens of the United States of America.* New York: Isaac Collins and Son. 1803. 11 pp.

Williams, John, *A Discourse, Delivered April 5, 1803, in the Baptist Church, in Gold-street.* New York: Isaac Collins and Son. 1803. 30 pp.

Barbauld, Anna Letitia (Aikin), *Hymns in Prose for Children.* 6th Edition. New York: Isaac Collins and Son, 1804. 96 pp.

Bible Stories. New York: Collins and Son. 1804. 257 pp.

Delacoste, J. B., *Catalogue of the Natural Productions and Curiosities . . . of the Cabinet of Natural History.* New York: Isaac Collins and Son. 1804. 87 pp.

Lancaster, Joseph, *Improvements in Education.* New York: Isaac Collins and Son. 1804. 39 pp.

Mavor, William Fordyce, *Universal History, Ancient and Modern; from the Earliest Records of Time, to the General Peace of 1801,* Vols. I, V, VIII, X, XII, XIV, XV, XVII, XIX, XXI. New York: Isaac Collins and Son. 1804.

——, *Universal History,* etc., Vols. XXIII, XXV. New York: Isaac Collins and Son. 1805.

New-York Hospital, *A Brief Account of the New-York Hospital.* New York: Isaac Collins and Son. 1804. 39 pp.

Otis, Harrison Gray, *Eulogy on General Alexander Hamilton.* New York: Isaac Collins and Son. 1804. 23 pp.

Rice, David, *Slavery Inconsistent with Justice and Good Policy.* New York: Isaac Collins and Son. 1804. 36 pp.

Schlabrendorf, Gustav, graf von, *Bonaparte, and the French People Under His Consulate.* 1st American Edition. New York: Isaac Collins and Son. 1804. 379 pp.

Bevan, Joseph Gurney, *A Summary of the History, Doctrine, and Discipline of Friends.* New York: Collins, Perkins & Co. 1805. 28 pp.

A Catalogue of Books and Stationery, for Sale by Collins, Perkins & Co. New York. 1805. 24 pp.

Dwight, Timothy, *A Sermon on Duelling.* New York: Collins, Perkins & Co. 1805. 38 pp.

Grahame, James, *The Sabbath.* 1st American Edition. New York: Collins, Perkins & Co. 1805. 168 pp.

Murray, Lindley, *An Abridgement of . . . English Grammar.* New York: Isaac Collins. 1805.

——, *English Grammar.* 3rd Edition. New York: Collins, Perkins & Co. 1805.

New-York Missionary Society, *Report . . . April 1st, 1805.* New York: Collins, Perkins & Co. 1805. 11 pp.

Smith, Frederick, *On Fashion.* New York: Collins, Perkins & Co. 1805. 8 pp.

Tuke, Henry, *The Principles of Religion.* New York: Collins, Perkins & Co. 1805. 142 pp.

Woolman, John, *Serious Considerations on Various Subjects of Importance.* [Bound with the following works by the same author.] New York: Collins, Perkins & Co. 1805. Pp. 1–24.

———, *Considerations on the True Harmony of Mankind.* New York: Collins, Perkins & Co. 1805. Pp. 25–58.

———, *An Epistle to the Quarterly and Monthly Meetings of Friends.* New York: Collins, Perkins & Co. 1805. Pp. 59–81.

———, *Remarks on Sundry Subjects.* New York: Collins, Perkins & Co. 1805. Pp. 83–119.

———, *Some Expressions of John Woolman in His Last Illness.* New York: Collins, Perkins & Co. 1805. Pp. 121–128.

———, *A Word of Remembrance and Caution to the Rich.* New York: Collins, Perkins & Co. 1805. Pp. 129–174.

The Holy Bible. 2nd Edition. [O.T. 1806, N.T. 1807.] New York: Collins, Perkins & Co.

Murray, Lindley, *The English Reader,* etc. New York: Collins, Perkins & Co. 1806. 356 pp.

Ostervald, Jean Frederic, *Practical Observations on the Old and New Testaments.* [Issued with Collins's Bible of 1806–1807.] New York: Collins, Perkins & Co.

Ricketson, Shadrach, *Means of Preserving Health, and Preventing Diseases.* New York: Collins, Perkins & Co. 1806. 298 pp.

Bard, Samuel, *A Compendium of the Theory and Practice of Midwifery.* New York: Collins and Perkins. 1807.

Catalogue of Medical and Chemical Books, for Sale by Collins and Perkins (Printers to the New-York Hospital, and importers of medical books for its library. New York. 1807. 15 pp.

GOVERNMENT
VOLUMES

New Jersey, *Acts of the General Assembly* (Oct. 10–Dec. 6, 1769). Burlington: Isaac Collins. 1770. 123 pp.

———, *Votes and Proceedings of the General Assembly* (3rd Session, 21st Assembly, Perth Amboy, Sept. 26–Oct. 27, 1770). Burlington: Isaac Collins. 1770. 53 pp.

New Jersey, *Votes and Proceedings of the General Assembly* (4th Session, 21st Assembly, Burlington, Apr. 17–Dec. 21, 1771). Burlington: Isaac Collins. 1771. 79 pp.

———, *Extracts from the Minutes and Proceedings of the Assembly, Relative to the Robbery of the Eastern Treasury.* Burlington: Isaac Collins. 1772. 32 pp.

———, *Votes and Proceedings of the General Assembly* (1st Session, 22nd Assembly, Perth Amboy, Aug. 19–Sept. 26, 1772). Burlington: Isaac Collins. 1772. 105 pp.

———, *A Bill in the Chancery . . . Robert Barclay, Against William, Earl of Stirling,* etc. Burlington: Isaac Collins. 1773. 51 pp.

———, *A Bill in the Chancery . . . Samuel Smith . . . Against Archibald Kennedy,* etc. Burlington: Isaac Collins. 1773. 11 pp.

———, *Votes and Proceedings of the General Assembly* (2nd Session, 22nd Assembly, Burlington, Nov. 10, 1773–Mar. 11, 1774). Burlington: Isaac Collins. 1774. 215 pp.

———, *Extracts from the Journal of Proceedings of the Provincial Congress* (May, June, August 1775, Trenton). Burlington: Isaac Collins. 1775. 44 pp.

———, *Journal of the Votes and Proceedings of the Provincial Congress* (Oct. 1775, Trenton). Burlington: Isaac Collins. 1775. 78 pp.

———, *Votes and Proceedings of the General Assembly* (3rd Session, 22nd Assembly, Perth Amboy, Jan. 11–Feb. 13, 1775). Burlington: Isaac Collins. 1775. 62 pp.

———, *Votes and Proceedings of the General Assembly* (1st Sitting, 4th Session, 22nd Assembly, Burlington, May 15–20, 1775). Burlington: Isaac Collins. 1775. 31 pp.

———, *Votes and Proceedings of the General Assembly* (2nd Sitting, 4th Session, 22nd Assembly, Burlington, Nov. 15–Dec. 6, 1775). Burlington: Isaac Collins. 1775. 39 pp.

———, *Acts of the General Assembly* (Apr. 17, 1702–Jan. 14, 1776). Compiled and published . . . by Samuel Allinson. Burlington: Isaac Collins. 1776. 531 pp.

———, *Constitution of New-Jersey.* Burlington: Isaac Collins. 1776. 12 pp.

———, *Journal of the Votes and Proceedings of the Convention of New-Jersey* (June 10–Aug. 21, 1776, Burlington, Trenton, New Brunswick). Burlington: Isaac Collins. 1776. 150 pp.

———, *A Letter* from William Franklin to the New-Jersey Assembly and Council stating the events leading to his expulsion as governor, June 22, 1776. Burlington: Isaac Collins. 1776. 3 pp.

———, *An Ordinance* for regulating the militia . . . To which is annexed the Continental articles of war. Burlington: Isaac Collins. 1776. 35 pp.

———, *An Act* for the better regulating of the militia, etc. Burlington: Isaac Collins. 1777. 14 pp.

New Jersey, *Acts of the General Assembly* (Aug. 27, 1776–Oct. 11, 1777). Burlington: Isaac Collins. 1777. Pp. 48, 49–80, 81–128.

———, *Journal of the Proceedings of the Legislative Council* (Aug. 27, 1776–June 7, 1777). Burlington: Isaac Collins. 1777. 95 pp.

———, *Speech* by Governor Livingston before the Council and the General Assembly, Feb. 25, 1777, Haddonfield. Burlington: Isaac Collins. 1777. 4 pp.

———, *Votes and Proceedings of the General Assembly* (Begun Aug. 27, 1776). Burlington: Isaac Collins. 1777. 148 pp.

———, *Acts of the General Assembly* (2nd Session, Oct. 28, 1777–Oct. 8, 1778). Burlington and Trenton: Isaac Collins. 1778. Pp. 26, 27–84, 85–91, 93–109.

———, *Acts of the General Assembly* (3rd Session, begun Oct. 27, 1778) Trenton: Isaac Collins. 1779. Pp. 45, 47–124, 125–139.

———, *Journal of the Proceedings of the Legislative Council* (Last Sitting, 1st Session, Sept. 3–Oct. 11, 1777). Trenton: Isaac Collins. 1779. Pp. 97–126.

———, *Journal of the Proceedings of the Legislative Council* (2nd Session, Oct. 28, 1777–Oct. 8, 1778). Trenton: Isaac Collins. 1779. 114 pp.

———, *Votes and Proceedings of the General Assembly* (Last Sitting, 1st Session, Sept. 3–Oct. 11, 1777). Trenton: Isaac Collins. 1779. Pp. 4, 153–206.

———, *Votes and Proceedings of the General Assembly* (2nd Session, Oct. 28, 1777–Oct. 8, 1778). Trenton: Isaac Collins. 1779. 204 pp.

———, *Votes and Proceedings of the General Assembly* (3rd Session, Oct. 27, 1778–Oct. 9, 1779). Trenton: Isaac Collins. 1779. Pp. 64, 65–156, 157–208.

———, *Acts of the General Assembly.* (4th Assembly, Oct. 26, 1779–Oct. 7, 1780). Trenton: Isaac Collins. 1780. Pp. 54, 55–78, 79–126, 126–139.

———, *Journal of the Proceedings of the Legislative Council* (3rd Session, Oct. 27, 1778–Oct. 7, 1780). Trenton: Isaac Collins. 1780. 106 pp.

———, *Journal of the Proceedings of the Legislative Council* (4th Session, Oct. 26, 1779–Oct. 7, 1780). Trenton: Isaac Collins. 1780. Pp. 46, 47–73, 75–126.

———, *Minutes and Proceedings of the Council and General Assembly in Joint-Meeting* (Aug. 30, 1776–May 1780). Trenton: Isaac Collins. 1780. 34 pp.

———, *Votes and Proceedings of the General Assembly* (4th Assembly, Oct. 26, 1779–Oct. 7, 1780). Trenton: Isaac Collins. 1780. Pp. 112, 113–182, 183–252, 263–299.

———, *Votes and Proceedings of the Fifth General Assembly* (Oct. 24–Dec. 15, 1780). Trenton: Isaac Collins. 1780. Pp. 8, 9–16, 17–24, 25–31, 34–40, 41–47, 48–52, 53–60.

New Jersey, *Acts of the Fifth General Assembly* (Oct. 24, 1780–Oct. 6, 1781). Trenton: Isaac Collins. 1781. Pp. 67, 69–118, 119–136.

———, *Journal of the Proceedings of the Legislative Council* (5th Session, Oct. 24, 1780–Oct. 6, 1781). 2 Vols. Trenton: Isaac Collins. 1781. 72, 50 pp.

———, *Votes and Proceedings of the General Assembly* (Dec. 16, 1780–Jan. 9, 1781). Trenton: Isaac Collins. 1781. Pp. 61–108.

———, *Votes and Proceedings of the Fifth General Assembly* (2nd Sitting, May 15–June 28, 1781). Trenton: Isaac Collins. 1781. 102 pp.

———, *Votes and Proceedings of the Fifth General Assembly* (3rd Sitting, Sept. 10–Oct. 6, 1781). Trenton: Isaac Collins. 1781. 34 pp.

———, *Acts of the Sixth General Assembly* (Oct. 23, 1781–Oct. 5, 1782). Trenton: Isaac Collins. 1782. Pp. 61, 63–114, 115–126.

———, *Journal of the Proceedings of the Legislative Council* (6th Session, Oct. 23, 1781–Oct. 5, 1782). 2 Vols. Trenton: Isaac Collins. 1782. 37, 39 pp.

———, *Votes and Proceedings of the Sixth General Assembly* (Oct. 23, 1781–Oct. 5, 1782). 3 Vols. Trenton: Isaac Collins. 1782. 81, 50, 24 pp.

———, *Acts of the Seventh General Assembly* (Begun Oct. 22, 1782). Trenton: Isaac Collins. 1783. Pp. 28, 29–77.

———, *Journal of the Proceedings of the Legislative Council* (1st and 2nd Sittings, 7th Session, Oct. 22, 1782–June 19, 1783). Trenton: Isaac Collins. 1783. Pp. 38, 39–70.

———, *Minutes and Proceedings of the Council and General Assembly in Joint-Meeting* (June 17, 1780–Dec. 20, 1783). Trenton: Isaac Collins. 1783. Pp. 41–60.

———, *Votes and Proceedings of the Seventh General Assembly* (1st and 2nd Sittings, Oct. 22, 1782–June 19, 1783). Trenton: Isaac Collins. 1783. Pp. 89, 91–150.

United States of America, *Address and Recommendations to the States . . . in Congress Assembled.* Trenton: Isaac Collins. 1783. 56 pp.

New Jersey, *Acts of the Council and General Assembly . . . from the Establishment of the Present Government . . . to the First Sitting of the Eighth Session, on the 24th Day of December, 1783.* Peter Wilson, compiler. Trenton: Isaac Collins. 1784. 455 pp.

———, *Acts of the Eighth General Assembly* (Oct. 28–Dec. 24, 1783). Trenton: Isaac Collins. 1784. Pp. 72, 75–121.

———, *Acts of the Ninth General Assembly* (Begun Oct. 26, 1784). Trenton: Isaac Collins. 1784. Pp. 125–186.

———, *Journal of the Proceedings of the Legislative Council.* (1st Sitting, 8th Session, begun Oct. 28, 1783). Trenton: Isaac Collins. 1784. 52 pp.

New Jersey, *Journal of the Preceedings of the Legislative Council* (2nd Sitting, 8th Session, begun Aug. 5, 1784). Trenton: Isaac Collins. 1784. 26 pp.

——, *Votes and Proceedings of the Eighth General Assembly* (Begun Oct. 28, 1783). Trenton: Isaac Collins. 1784. 90 pp.

——, *Votes and Proceedings of the Ninth General Assembly* (Begun Oct. 26, 1784). Trenton: Isaac Collins. 1784. 101 pp.

——, *An Act for Incorporating the Free Port of Perth-Amboy* (Passed Dec. 21, 1784). Trenton: Isaac Collins. 1785. 24 pp.

——, *Acts of the Tenth General Assembly* (1st Sitting, begun Oct. 25, 1785). Trenton: Isaac Collins. 1785. Pp. 191–230.

——, *Journal of the Proceedings of the Legislative Council* (1st Sitting, 9th Session, begun Oct. 26, 1784). Trenton: Isaac Collins. 1785. 53 pp.

——, *Journal of the Proceedings of the Legislative Council* (1st Sitting, 10th Session, begun Oct. 25, 1785). Trenton: Isaac Collins. 1785. 37 pp.

——, *Votes and Proceedings of the Tenth General Assembly* (1st Sitting, begun Oct. 25, 1785). Trenton: Isaac Collins. 1785. 83 pp.

——, *Acts of the Tenth General Assembly* (2nd and 3rd Sittings). Trenton: Isaac Collins. 1786. Pp. 235–288, 293–334.

——, *Acts of the Eleventh General Assembly* (Begun Oct. 24, 1786, 1st Sitting). Trenton: Isaac Collins. 1786. Pp. 337–383.

——, *Journal of the Proceedings of the Legislative Council* (2nd Sitting, 10th Session, begun Feb. 15, 1786). Trenton: Isaac Collins. 1786. 48 pp.

——, *Journal of the Proceedings of the Legislative Council* (3rd Sitting, 10th Session, begun May 17, 1786). Trenton: Isaac Collins. 1786. 16 pp.

——, *Journal of the Proceedings of the Legislative Council* (1st Sitting, 11th Session, begun Oct. 24, 1786). Trenton: Isaac Collins. 1786. 36 pp.

——, *Votes and Proceedings of the Tenth General Assembly* (2nd Sitting). Trenton: Isaac Collins. 1786. 87 pp.

——, *Votes and Proceedings of the Eleventh General Assembly* (1st Sitting, begun Oct. 24, 1786). Trenton: Isaac Collins. 1786. 76 pp.

——, *Acts of the Eleventh General Assembly* (2nd Sitting). Trenton: Isaac Collins. 1786. Pp. 387–435.

——, *Acts of the Twelfth General Assembly* (Begun Oct. 23, 1787). Trenton: Isaac Collins. 1787. Pp. 439–452.

——, *Journal of the Proceedings of the Legislative Council* (2nd Sitting, 11th Session). Trenton: Isaac Collins. 1787. 26 pp.

——, *Journal of the Proceedings of the Legislative Council* (Begun Oct. 23, 1787). Trenton: Isaac Collins. 1787. 26 pp.

New Jersey, *Votes and Proceedings of the Eleventh General Assembly* (2nd Sitting). Trenton: Isaac Collins. 1787. 44 pp.

———, *Votes and Proceedings of the Twelfth General Assembly* (Begun Oct. 23, 1787). Trenton: Isaac Collins. 1787. 66 pp.

United States of America, *The Constitution . . . Agreed to in Convention, at Philadelphia, Sept. 17, 1787*. Trenton: Isaac Collins. 1787. 16 pp.

New Jersey, *Acts of the Twelfth General Assembly* (2nd Sitting). Trenton: Isaac Collins. 1788. Pp. 455–470.

———, *Acts of the Thirteenth General Assembly* (Begun Oct. 28, 1788, 1st Sitting). Trenton: Isaac Collins. 1788. Pp. 473–514.

———, *Journal of the Proceedings of the Legislative Council* (2nd Sitting, 12th Session). Trenton: Isaac Collins. 1788. 18 pp.

———, *Journal of the Proceedings of the Legislative Council* (Begun Oct. 28, 1788). Trenton: Isaac Collins. 1788. 35 pp.

———, *Minutes of the Convention of the State of New-Jersey* (Convened Dec. 11, 1787, to ratify U.S. Constitution). Trenton: Isaac Collins. 1788. 31 pp.

———, *Votes and Proceedings of the Twelfth General Assembly* (2nd Sitting). Trenton: Isaac Collins. 1788. 33 pp.

———, *Votes and Proceedings of the Thirteenth General Assembly* (Begun Oct. 1788, 1st Sitting). Trenton: Isaac Collins. 1788. 103 pp.

United States of America, *The Memorial of the Publick Creditors, Citizens of the State of New-Jersey*. Trenton: Isaac Collins. 1790. 16 pp.

New Jersey, *Acts of the Seventeenth General Assembly* (Begun Oct. 23, 1792, 1st Sitting). Trenton: Isaac Collins. 1792. Pp. 783–829.

———, *Acts of the Seventeenth General Assembly* (2nd Sitting). Trenton: Isaac Collins. 1793. Pp. 833–870.

———, *Journal of the Proceedings of the Legislative Council* (1st and 2nd Sittings, 17th Session). 2 Vols. Trenton: Isaac Collins. 1793. 44, 29 pp.

———, *Votes and Proceedings of the Seventeenth General Assembly* (Begun Oct. 23, 1792, 1st Sitting). Trenton: Isaac Collins. 1793. 98 pp.

———, *An Act for Regulating Roads and Bridges* (Supplement to the act) Trenton: Isaac Collins. 1794. 4 pp.

———, *Acts of the Eighteenth General Assembly* (Begun Oct. 22, 1793, 1st and 2nd Sittings). Trenton: Isaac Collins. 1794. Pp. 875–914.

———, *Journal of the Proceedings of the Legislative Council* (3rd Sitting, 18th Session). Trenton: Isaac Collins. 1794. 12 pp.

———, *Journal of the Proceedings of the Legislative Council* (1st and 2nd Sittings, 19th Session). 2 Vols. Trenton: Isaac Collins. 1795. 36, 48 pp.

———, *Votes and Proceedings of the Twentieth General Assembly* (Begun Oct. 27, 1795, 1st Sitting). Trenton: Isaac Collins. 1795. 86 pp.

———, *Votes and Proceedings of the Twentieth General Assembly* (2nd Sitting). Trenton: Isaac Collins. 1796. 66 pp.

New York, *Collection of Penal Laws, and Laws Concerning the State Prison.* New York: Isaac Collins. 1799.

——, *Term Reports of Cases Argued and Determined in the Supreme Court of New-York.* Vol. I, Pt. I. New York: Isaac Collins and Son. 1803.

BROADSIDES

New Jersey, A proclamation proroguing the Assembly. Burlington: Isaac Collins. 1770.

Wake, Baldwin, A message to Samuel Allinson concerning the indenture of a free Negro, Dec. 17, 1774. Burlington: Isaac Collins. 1774.

New Jersey, An address to the Governor from the Council expressing allegiance to the Crown and the Governor's reply. Burlington: Isaac Collins. 1775.

——, An address to the Governor from the General Assembly resolving to support Great Britain and the Governor's answer. Burlington: Isaac Collins. 1775.

——, A message to the Council from Governor William Franklin, Dec. 6, 1775. Burlington: Isaac Collins. 1775.

——, A message to the Governor from the Council, Dec. 4, 1775. Burlington: Isaac Collins. 1775.

——, A circular letter from Governor William Livingston calling upon the militia to emulate their brethren in South Carolina, Nov. 1776. Burlington: Isaac Collins. 1776.

——, Governor Livingston's circular letter to the colonels of militia. Burlington, Nov. 24, 1776.

——, Provincial Congress resolution that five battalions be readied and marched to New-York, by order of Congress, Samuel Tucker, president. Burlington, June 14, 1776.

——, An appeal from General Washington and Governor Livingston to the militia to repel the British, Trenton, Nov. 23, 1777. Burlington: Isaac Collins. 1777.

——, An act for compleating the quota of troops belonging to this state in the service of the United States, Trenton, Mar. 11, 1780.

——, An act to compleat the three regiments of this state in the service of the United States, and to raise a company of volunteers for the defence of part of the county of Monmouth. Passed June 14, 1780. Trenton: Isaac Collins. 1780.

——, Proclamation appointing the second Thursday of December, 1783, . . . as a day of public thanksgiving for the restoration of peace. Trenton, Nov. 11, 1783. Signed, Wm. Livingston, Isaac Collins.

New Jersey, Proclamation from Governor Livingston recommending to the people of the United States a day of public thanksgiving and prayer. Trenton: Isaac Collins. 1789.

Reinagle, Alexander, A Sonata, sung by a number of young girls . . . As General Washington passed under the triumphal arch raised on the bridge at Trenton, April 21, 1789.

Collins, Isaac, Notice . . . to the public in general, and in particular to the subscribers to the edition of the Holy Scriptures . . . that . . . it will be finished by the first day of the tenth month next. Sept. 1, 1791.

Society of Friends, Extract from the epistle of the Meeting for sufferings in London, July 7, 1751. Re-published by directions of a Meeting for sufferings, Philadelphia, Dec. 15, 1791. Trenton: Isaac Collins. 1791.

New Jersey, An act to prevent persons, holding shares of propriety, from cutting timber on the unlocated lands in this state. Passed Feb. 10, 1794. Trenton: Isaac Collins. 1794.

Company of Master Builders, Whereas experience has shewn that much irregularity and confusion has taken place . . . meeting held March 11, 1805. New York: Isaac Collins and Son. 1805.

NOTES

ᴥᴥ I ᴥᴥ

APPRENTICE

1 Frederick B. Tolles, *Meeting House and Counting House: The Quaker Merchants of Colonial Philadelphia, 1682–1763* (Chapel Hill, N.C., 1948), p. 29.

2 Sydney V. James, *A People Among Peoples: Quaker Benevolence in Eighteenth-Century America* (Cambridge, Mass., 1963), p. 3.

3 John A. Munroe, *Federalist Delaware, 1775–1815* (New Brunswick, N.J., 1954), p. 28.

4 *Reminiscences of Isaac and Rachel (Budd) Collins* (Philadelphia, 1893), pp. 7–8. Written to William Dillwyn and dated April 24, 1774, the letter reads:

"After my father's decease his widow married again and removed into a remote part of the country from where I dwelt, and I have not seen her for fourteen years, nor since I have had a desire for correspondence with some of my uncles or cousins, and by that means I have been prevented from getting a good traditional knowledge.

"I cannot call all my uncles by name, nor am I certain of the number, but, according to the best of my remembrance, my father's eldest brother's name was John Collins, who, after the death of his father, was entrusted with the care of his brethren, and by whom my father was put out an apprentice to a wine-cooper in Bristol, England. I think I have been told that I had an uncle name Robert and another William, and after the last mentioned my brother William had his name. My father had a brother who followed the sea—was captain or commander of a vessel which had sailed to New York, and for aught I know was in that trade. He had a liberal education in the Episcopal Church. He has been dead about twenty-one years.

"As I have but few relations by my mother's side, and as I conceive there is great pleasure in having an acquaintance with both, I am thus solicitous, which I hope will be sufficient apology for my requesting thee to take some pains in this matter."

This book also notes: "The parents of Isaac Collins, both of whom belonged to the Society of Friends, died during his child-hood, and little is known of his family from the fact stated in one of his letters that the family records were destroyed by fire."

5 Taken from Isaiah Thomas's indenture, dated 1756, as reprinted in Annie Russell Marble, *From 'Prentice to Patron* (New York, 1935), pp. 9–10.

6 August Klapper, *The Printer in Eighteenth-Century Williamsburg* (Williamsburg, 1964), p. 6.

7 Isaiah Thomas, *The History of Printing in America,* 2nd ed. (Albany, 1874), I, 319.

8 Dorothy Lawson Hawkins, "James Adams: The First Printer of Delaware," *Papers of the Bibliographical Society of America,* XXVIII (1934); and Douglas McMurtrie, "Delaware Imprints of 1761," *American Book Collector,* August-September, 1932.

9 *Ibid.*

10 Thomas, II, 154.

11 Anon., "Journal of a French Traveller in the Colonies, 1765," *American Historical Review,* XXVI (July, 1921), 742–743. See also Wilson Smith, ed., *Cities of Our Past and Present* (New York, 1964), p. 23.

12 Hugh Jones, *The Present State of Virginia . . .* (New York, 1865), pp. 25–32. See modern edition edited by Richard L. Morton (Chapel Hill, N.C., 1956), pp. 66–71, and Wilson Smith, pp. 18–22.

13 David Ramsay, *The History of the American Revolution* (Philadelphia, 1789), I, 61–62. Also see Arthur M. Schlesinger, *Prelude to Independence: The Newspaper War on Britain 1764–1776,* paperback ed. (New York, 1965), pp. 67–84.

14 Thomas, I, 336.

15 J. C. Oswald, *Benjamin Franklin, Printer* (Garden City, 1917); Thomas, I, 335–336; and Schlesinger, p. 79.

16 For a contemporary estimate of Philadelphia see William Birch & Son, *Views of Philadelphia,* a book of twenty-eight plates drawn and engraved between 1798 and 1800, published in 1802. Also see Thomas Jefferson Wertenbaker, *The Founding of American Civilization: The Middle Colonies* (New York, 1938), pp. 231–255.

17 For details on the *Pennsylvania Chronicle* and its publisher see Ward L. Miner, *William Goddard, Newspaperman* (Durham, N.C., 1962).

18 Hawkins, p. 63.

19 Miner, p. 206.

20 Minutes, Philadelphia Monthly Meeting, Department of Records, Philadelphia Yearly Meeting, Religious Society of Friends, 302 Arch Street, Philadelphia, pp. 367, 371.

21 For the output of the partnership see Charles R. Hildeburn, *A Century of Printing: The Issues of the Press in Pennsylvania, 1685–1784* (Philadelphia, 1775–1886), II, 88–122.

22 Quoted in Frederick B. Tolles, *Quakers and the Atlantic Culture* (New York, 1960), pp. 62–64.

◄§ II §►
MASTER PRINTER

1 *Archives of the State of New Jersey: Documents Relating to the Colonial History of the State of New Jersey,* ed. Frederick W. Ricord and William Nelson, First Series, x (Newark, 1886), 442. (Hereafter *New Jersey Archives.*)

2 Quoted in *Pennsylvania Magazine of History and Biography* (hereafter *PMHB*), XXIII (1899), 531. See also Frederick B. Tolles, "A Literary Quaker: John Smith of Burlington and Philadelphia," *PMHB*, LXV, 300–333.

3 Alfred Owen Aldridge, *Benjamin Franklin: Philosopher and Man* (Philadelphia and New York, 1965), pp. 71–72.

4 Letter to William Strahan dated October 27, 1753, from Philadelphia. *The Papers of Benjamin Franklin,* ed. Leonard Labaree, et al. (New Haven, 1962), V, 82–83.

5 Lawrence C. Wroth, *The Colonial Printer* (Portland, 1938), pp. 122–153. For Franklin's record of payment to Caslon see *The Papers of Benjamin Franklin* (New Haven, 1966), IX, 34n.

6 Milton Drake, compiler, *Almanacs of the United States* (New York, 1962), Preface.

7 *Ibid.*

8 For legislative details on Collins's appointment see *Votes and Proceedings of the General Assembly, September 26 to October 27, 1770* (Burlington, N.J., 1770).

9 The commission is reproduced in *Reminiscences of Isaac and Rachel (Budd) Collins* (Philadelphia, 1893), pp. 11–12.

10 *The Autobiography of Benjamin Franklin,* ed. Leonard W. Labaree, et al. (New Haven, 1964), p. 171. See also Daniel J. Boorstin, "The Publick Printer," *The Americans: The Colonial Experience* (New York, 1958), pp. 335–340.

11 Howard M. Jones, "The Importation of French Books in Philadelphia, 1750–1800," *Modern Philology*, XXXII (1934), 160. Also see Tolles, *PMHB*, LXV, 300–333.

12 William M. Sale, Jr., *Samuel Richardson: Master Printer* (Ithaca, 1950), pp. 86.

13 Quoted in Sale, p. 6.

14 Wroth, pp. 239–240. For a discussion of the importance of the pamphlet to early America see Bernard Bailyn, "The Literature of Revolution," *The Ideological Origins of the American Revolution* (Cambridge, Mass., 1967), pp. 1–21.

15 Frank Luther Mott, *Golden Multitudes: The Story of Best Sellers in the United States* (New York, 1947), pp. 31–32.

16 Minutes, Philadelphia Monthly Meeting, Department of Records, Philadelphia Yearly Meeting, Religious Society of Friends, 302 Arch Street, Philadelphia, pp. 439, 443.

17 Dated May 20–27, 1771.

18 *Reminiscences,* p. 38.

19 Tolles, *PMHB,* LXV, 304.

20 Quoted in Sydney V. James, *A People Among Peoples: Quaker Benevolence in Eighteenth-Century America* (Cambridge, Mass., 1963), p. 218.

21 James, p. 226.

22 *Ibid.,* p. 216. Note ch. XII, "Justice to the Negro."

23 *Ibid.,* p. 252. See also Minutes, Meeting for Sufferings, Philadelphia Yearly Meeting, pp. 359–360.

24 Collins to Pemberton, June 22, 1772, Historical Society of Pennsylvania (hereafter HSP).

25 Collins to Pemberton, January 4, 1773, HSP.

26 Aitken's "Waste Book, 1771–1802," Library Company of Philadelphia.

27 *Ibid.*

28 James, pp. 252–253.

29 Wroth, *Colonial Printer,* p. 151.

30 Collins to Pemberton, January 4, 1773, HSP.

31 Wroth, *Colonial Printer,* pp. 149–150.

32 *Pennsylvania Packet,* January 25, 1773; *Pennsylvania Gazette,* August 4, 1773.

33 "Prices of Printing Work in Philadelphia, 1754," by Benjamin Franklin, American Antiquarian Society Library, quoted by Wroth, *Colonial Printer,* p. 162.

34 Isaiah Thomas, *The History of Printing in America,* 2nd ed. (Albany, 1874), I, 142–144, 260.

35 George A. Kubler, *A New History of Stereotyping* (New York, 1941), p. 148; Thomas, I, 144.

36 *Votes and Proceedings of the General Assembly, November 10, 1773, to March 11, 1774* (Burlington, N.J., 1774), pp. 206–207.

37 *Journal of the Votes and Proceedings of the . . . Provincial Congress, January 31 to March 2, 1776* (New York, 1776), p. 51.

38 An obscure New York printer, John Anderson, printed the *Journal* of the New Jersey Provincial Congress for the sitting at New Brunswick from January 31 to March 2, 1776. There is no explanation

for Collins not getting this assignment, other than the confused nature of government at the time. Collins printed the *Journal of the Provincial Congress* which met in Trenton in October 1775 and the *Journal* of the New Jersey convention begun at Burlington on June 10, 1776, and continued at Trenton and New Brunswick through August 21. Perhaps the main reason for employing another printer during this brief transitional period was the ambivalence of Collins's position as "public printer." But once the change in governments was completed, Collins resumed his role as official legislative printer.

39 Collins's account with New Jersey is in the library of the Historical Society of Pennsylvania.

40 Frederick B. Tolles, *Meeting House and Counting House: The Quaker Merchants of Colonial Philadelphia, 1682–1763* (Chapel Hill, N.C., 1948).

41 Printed in "Notes and Queries," *PMHB*, XVIII (1894), 260.

42 See Donald L. Kemmerer, *Path to Freedom: The Struggle for Self-Government in Colonial New Jersey, 1703–1776* (Princeton, 1949), p. 343.

43 *New Jersey Archives*, First Series, X, 731.

ᵛᵍ III ᵍᵛ
NEWSPAPER
PUBLISHER

1 If we assume that the *Wilmington Courant* did not become a reality in
   or about 1762 (see Chap. I), Delaware was the last of the original
   colonies to have a newspaper. The "first" newspaper in Delaware
   was the *Delaware Gazette,* established in 1785 in Wilmington,
   eight years after New Jersey got its first paper. This list of thirty-
   eight newspapers includes the *Boston Post-Boy,* which ended publication on April 17, 1775, two days before the battles of Lexington
   and Concord.

2 For another interpretation of Rivington see Catherine Snell Crary,
   "The Tory and the Spy: The Double Life of James Rivington,"
   William and Mary Quarterly, XVI (January, 1959), 61–72.

3 Lyon N. Richardson, *A History of Early American Magazines, 1741–
   1784* (New York, 1931), p. 123.

4 Quoted in Richardson, pp. 123–135.

5 Richardson, p. 128.

6 Richardson, p. 135.

7 William Nelson, "Some New Jersey Printers and Printing in the
   Eighteenth Century," *Proceedings of the American Antiquarian
   Society,* New Series, XXI (1911), 25.

8 Printed in Ward L. Miner, *William Goddard, Newspaperman* (Durham, N.C., 1962), pp. 50–51.

9 Major W. I. Lincoln, "New Jersey's Tea Party," *Proceedings of the
   New Jersey Historical Society,* New Series, X (April, 1925), 170.

10 A contemporaneous copy, written by Thomas Harris of Bridgeton, is in
   the Special Collections, Rutgers University Library, which also
   has two copies of the privately printed edition of 1894, with an
   introduction and notes by William Nelson.

11 *Diary and Autobiography of John Adams,* ed. L. H. Butterfield (Cambridge, Mass., 1961), II, 118–119, and Page Smith, *John Adams*
   (New York, 1962), I, 164.

12 Charles Angoff, *Literary History of the American People* (New York, 1931), I, 358–359.

13 *New-York Gazette and Weekly Mercury*, April 14, 1777.

14 February 15, 1777. *The Writings of Washington from the Original Manuscript Sources, 1745–1799*, ed. John C. Fitzpatrick (Washington, 1932).

15 *Ibid.*, February 22, 1777.

16 *Ibid.*, to Philip Livingston, Elbridge Gerry, and George Clymer, members of a special committee, July 19, 1777.

17 For the events leading up to the establishment of the *Gazette* see *Minutes of the Provincial Congress and the Council of Safety . . .* (Trenton, 1879) and *Selections from the Correspondence of the Executive of New Jersey, from 1776 to 1786* (Newark, 1848).

18 Quoted in Lawrence C. Wroth, *The Colonial Printer* (Portland, 1938), p. 105.

19 For the inventory and appraisement of the Rind shop see *William and Mary College Quarterly*, XVII (January, 1937), 53–55.

20 The "Proposals," in Collins's handwriting, are in the Rare Book Room, New York Public Library (hereafter NYPL).

21 Richard P. McCormick, *New Jersey from Colony to State—1609–1789* (Princeton, 1964), p. 143.

22 *Writings of Washington . . .*, February 22, 1778.

23 Quoted in Clarence S. Brigham, *Journals and Journeymen: A Contribution to the History of Early American Newspapers* (Philadelphia, 1950), p. 27.

24 Jackson Turner Main, *The Social Structure of Revolutionary America* (Princeton, 1965), p. 77. See also the numerous newspaper advertisements for the period.

25 See Carl Bridenbaugh, *The Colonial Craftsman* (New York, 1950), pp. 57–58, and Wheaton J. Lane, *From Indian Trail to Iron Horse* (Princeton, 1939), p. 66.

26 Quoted in Thomas F. Gordon, *A Gazetteer of the State of New Jersey* (Trenton, 1834), pp. 253–254.

27 *Votes and Proceedings of the General Assembly, October 28, 1777, to October 8, 1778* (Burlington, N.J., 1779), pp. 78, 80.

28 See Main, p. 289.

29 Livingston to Collins, February 22, 1779, Livingston Papers, Massachusetts Historical Society (hereafter MHS), on microfilm at Rutgers University Library.

30 See John R. Anderson, "The Rebel Press of Shepard Kollock, Chatham, 1779–1783" (unpublished master's thesis, New York University, 1961).

31 For the events of the disownment proceedings see the Minutes, Burlington Monthly Meeting, Department of Records, Philadelphia Yearly Meetings, Religious Society of Friends, 302 Arch Street, Philadelphia, pp. 192–197.

❧ IV ❧

NEWSPAPER EDITOR

1 Collins to Livingston, December 12, 1777, Livingston Papers, MHS.
2 Leonard W. Levy, *Legacy of Suppression: Freedom of Speech and Press in Early American History* (Cambridge, Mass., 1960), p. 18.
3 Livingston to Lee, January 16, 1779, Livingston Papers, MHS.
4 *New-Jersey Gazette,* June 17, 1780.
5 *Votes and Proceedings of the General Assembly, October 26, 1779, to October 7, 1780* (Trenton, 1780), p. 8.
6 Quoted in *Reminiscences of Isaac and Rachel (Budd) Collins* (Philadelphia, 1893), pp. 24–25.
7 For the Dunlap episodes I am indebted to Dwight L. Teeter, "Press Freedom and the Public Printing: Pennsylvania, 1775–1783," a paper presented at the History Division, Association for Education in Journalism Convention, Boulder, Colorado, August 29, 1967. Teeter adds: "Such suppressive powers resided in the legislatures of colonial America, which regarded themselves as miniature Parliaments. But Congress, dependent upon instructions from the legislatures or conventions of the states, was never given the power to punish speech and press during the War for Independence."
8 Livingston to Collins, February 22, 1779, Livingston Papers, MHS.
9 Collins to Livingston, March 6, 1781, Livingston Collection, NYPL.
10 Arthur M. Schlesinger, *Prelude to Independence: The Newspaper War on Britain, 1764–1776* (New York, 1958), p. 189.
11 See Wheaton J. Lane, *From Indian Trail to Iron Horse* (Princeton, 1939), p. 174.
12 See Arthur D. Pierce, *Iron in the Pines: The Story of New Jersey's Ghost Towns and Bog Iron* (New Brunswick, N.J., 1957), pp. 190–192.
13 Richard B. Morris, *The Peacemakers: The Great Powers and American Independence* (New York, 1965), p. 448.
14 *Ibid.*
15 Morris, p. 381.
16 Collins to Livingston, February 7, 1784, Livingston Papers, MHS.

17 Collins to Livingston, March 2, 1784, Livingston Papers, MHS.
18 *New-Jersey Gazette,* March 30, April 13, 20, 26, and May 3, 1784.
19 Quoted in Levy, *Legacy of Suppression,* p. 130.
20 *New-Jersey Gazette,* March 30, 1784.
21 *Legacy of Suppression,* pp. 224–225, 233.
22 Franklin to Francis Hopkinson, December 24, 1782, cited in Levy, p. 187n.
23 *Ibid.,* p. 182.
24 Alfred Owen Aldridge, *Benjamin Franklin: Philosopher and Man* (Philadelphia and New York, 1965), p. 73.
25 Kenneth Q. Jennings, "The Press of New Jersey," in *The Story of New Jersey,* ed. William Starr Myers (New York, 1945), II, Ch. III. See also Clarence S. Brigham, *History and Bibliography of American Newspapers, 1690–1820* (Worcester, Mass, 1947).
26 Samuel Miller, *A Brief Retrospect of the Eighteenth Century* (New York, 1803), II, 246.
27 Jennings, *loc. cit.*

⁓ V ⁔
MERCHANT
AND CITIZEN

1 Frederick B. Tolles, *Meeting House and Counting House: The Quaker Merchants of Colonial Philadelphia, 1682–1763* (Chapel Hill, N.C., 1948), p. 85.

2 *Reminiscences of Isaac and Rachel (Budd) Collins* (Philadelphia, 1893), p. 41.

3 William L. Dayton, *Historical Sketch of the Trenton Academy* (Trenton, 1881).

4 *Ibid.*

5 Charles Angoff, *Literary History of the American People* (New York, 1931), I, 358–359.

6 A Trenton Academy diploma, dated September 20, 1791, is in the Free Public Library of Trenton. It lists subjects studied at the Academy.

7 *Ibid.;* Dayton, *Historical Sketch.*

8 Nelson R. Burr, *Education in New Jersey, 1630–1871* (Princeton, 1942), pp. 193–194.

9 *Ibid.,* pp. 186–197.

10 Donald L. Kemmerer, *Path to Freedom: The Struggle for Self-Government in Colonial New Jersey, 1703–1776* (Princeton, 1940), p. 281.

11 Jackson Turner Main, *The Social Structure of Revolutionary America* (Princeton, 1965), pp. 87–88.

12 Letter from Du Simitière to Dr. William Bryant, Trenton, June 17, 1779, reprinted in *PMHB* (1889), XIII, 363.

13 Letter from Collins to James Thornton, June 4, 1790, Quaker Collection, Haverford College Library. David Brearly, mentioned in the letter, was chief justice of the New Jersey Supreme Court, 1779 to 1789, then became judge of the United States District Court in New Jersey. He served as a lieutenant colonel in the Revolution and was named a New Jersey representative to the Constitutional Convention in Philadelphia in 1787.

14 *Reminiscences,* p. 43.

15 The essay is in Collins's handwriting; Manuscript Room, Princeton
   University Library, AM 12437.
16 The second essay, also in Collins's own handwriting, is in the Quaker
   Collection, Haverford College Library.
17 Isaiah Thomas, *The History of Printing in America,* 2nd ed. (Albany,
   1874), I, 247–250.
18 *The Papers of Benjamin Franklin,* ed. Leonard W. Labaree et al.
   (New Haven, 1962), V, 421–422n; also see IV, 77, 484.
19 Thomas, I, 247–250.
20 *The Autobiography of Benjamin Franklin,* ed. Leonard W. Labaree,
   et al. (New Haven, 1964), p. 112; Lawrence C. Wroth, *The Colonial Printer* (Portland, 1938), p. 286.
21 See Paul Harvey, *The Oxford Companion to English Literature,* 3rd
   ed. (London, 1958), p. 636, for biographical information on Price.
22 Page Smith, *The Historian and History* (New York, 1964), p. 167. See
   also his chapter entitled "A Case in Point: the American Revolution."
23 Robert L. Brunhouse, "David Ramsay's Publication Problems, 1784–
   1808," *Papers of the Bibliographical Society of America,* XXXIX
   (1945).
24 *Ibid.*
25 The Trentoniana Collection in the Free Public Library, Trenton, has
   several of Collins's receipted bills, among them the charges for
   advertising in the *Gazette* the government sale of property once
   owned by Loyalists.
26 Dwight L. Teeter, "Press Freedom and the Public Printing: Pennsylvania, 1775–1783," a paper presented at the History Division,
   Association for Education in Journalism Convention, Boulder,
   Colorado, August 29, 1967.
27 The inquiry is in the Emlen Papers, Miscellaneous Letters, HSP.
28 Minutes, Burlington Monthly Meeting, Department of Records, Philadelphia Yearly Meeting, Religious Society of Friends, 302 Arch
   Street, Philadelphia, p. 143.
29 A period of silence, a Quaker custom.
30 Minutes, Chesterfield Monthly Meeting, Department of Records, Philadelphia Yearly Meeting.

►§ VI §◄
THE COLLINS BIBLE

1 For the history of Bible publishing in early America see Margaret T. Hills, *The English Bible in America* (New York, 1961); Edwin A. R. Rumball-Petre, *America's First Bibles* (Portland, Me., 1940); P. Marion Simms, *The Bible in America: Versions That Have Played Their Part in the Making of the Republic* (New York, 1936); John Wright, *Early Bibles in America* (New York, 1894); and Randolph G. Adams, "America's First Bibles," *The Colophon,* New Series 1 (Summer, 1935).

2 Isaiah Thomas, *The History of Printing in America,* 2nd ed. (Albany, 1874), I, 316.

3 Letter from Ramsay to Rev. Ashbel Green, Philadelphia, October 4, 1790, Boston Public Library, from a copy made by Carol Spawn of Philadelphia.

4 Livingston to Collins, September 11, 1788, reproduced in the printer's proposals, Huntington Library, San Marino, California.

5 George C. Rockefeller, "The First Testaments Printed in New Jersey," *Papers of the Bibliographical Society of America,* XLV (1951); William Nelson, *Issues of the New Jersey Press* (Paterson, 1899). While looking for the 1780 edition, Rockefeller "rediscovered" the 1779 edition in the Historical Society of Pennsylvania, where it had gone unnoticed since its acquisition in 1924. During the same hunt, Rockefeller located the 1782 edition in the Yale University Library.

6 Proposals pamphlet, Huntington Library.

7 Jackson Turner Main, *The Social Structure of Revolutionary America* (Princeton, 1965), p. 289. Also see Simon L. Adler, "Money and Money Units in the American Colonies," *Publications,* Rochester Historical Society (1929), VIII, 143–173; and Don Taxay, *The U.S. Mint and Coinage: An Illustrated History from 1776 to the Present* (New York, 1966), Part I. In 1785 the Continental Congress adopted the decimal ratio with the dollar as its unit. The British pound and the Spanish milled dollar, the "piece of eight,"

were still used as currency or as the basis of commercial calculations.

8   Livingston Papers, MHS.

9   Lawrence C. Wroth, "Book Production and Distribution from the Beginning to the War Between the States," in *The Book in America: A History of the Making, the Selling, and the Collecting of Books in the United States,* ed. Hellmut Lehmann-Haupt (New York, 1939), p. 48.

10   Collins's subscription plan for publishing Samuel Allinson's compilation of New Jersey laws appeared in the *Pennsylvania Gazette* for August 13, 1774.

11   Quoted in Simms, pp. 128–129.

12   Cited by Wroth in *The Book in America.* The Franklin & Hall Work Book for the years 1759–1766 is in the Manuscript Division, NYPL.

13   Simms, pp. 125–126.

14   Cited in Wright, p. 58.

15   *Ibid.,* pp. 66–67.

16   Simms, p. 127.

17   *Ibid.* Aitken's appeal and the denial of Congress were in 1789. After Aitken's Bible and before Collins's, William Woodhouse of Philadelphia "published" the *Christian's New and Complete Family Bible* in 1788 and 1790, but no copies have been located and there is doubt that it was printed in America. It was advertised as a folio edition. Also in 1790 William Young of Philadelphia issued a small "school edition" of the complete Bible. For details see Hills.

18   Minutes, Chesterfield Monthly Meeting, Department of Records, Philadelphia Yearly Meeting, Religious Society of Friends, 302 Arch Street, Philadelphia, p. 103.

19   Archives, New England Yearly Meeting of Friends, Providence, R.I.

20   Minutes, General Assembly of the Presbyterian Church in the U.S.A., Presbyterian Historical Society, Philadelphia.

21   Quoted from letter to the author from William B. Miller, assistant secretary, Presbyterian Historical Society, October 10, 1962.

22   *Reminiscences of Isaac and Rachel (Budd) Collins* (Philadelphia, 1893), p. 18.

23   Collins's proposals pamphlet, Huntington Library, p. 3.

24   Presbyterian Minutes, Presbyterian Historical Society.

25   Collins's proposals pamphlet, Huntington Library, p. 2.

26   Variations in content were observed in several copies of the Bible I examined. The one at Rutgers University, for example, does not contain Ostervald's *Notes,* but the one in the New Jersey State Library does. Both contain Downame's *Concordance,* but a copy in the Savitz Library, Glassboro State College, is without either.

27 *Reminiscences,* p. 20.

28 A copy of the broadside Collins released on September 1 is in the Boston Public Library. The same information appeared in the *Pennsylvania Gazette* for six weeks in October and November. On November 8 in the *Brunswick Gazette,* New Brunswick, New Jersey, he reported that "Subscriptions will be received until the last day of the twelfth month (December) next." Another piece of evidence is the date, August 1, 1792, which appears in an inscribed copy Collins presented to James Ewing "for his attention to correcting the press." It may be that Collins waited until he had satisfied subscribers before presenting free copies to helpful friends. This copy is now owned by Michael Papantonio of New York City.

29 How many bound copies Thomas was able to supply in December we do not know, but it seems unlikely that a bindery of that time could have produced many volumes in fourteen days, that is, the same length of time he had allowed for the folio. For more information see Clifford K. Shipton, *Isaiah Thomas: Printer, Patriot and Philanthropist, 1749-1831* (Rochester, 1948), pp. 58–59.

30 Simms, p. 130.

31 As printed in the copy in the Savitz Library, Glassboro State College, Glassboro, N.J.

32 Quoted in C. Clement Samford, *The Bookbinder in Eighteenth-Century Williamsburg* (Williamsburg, 1964), p. 29.

33 *Reminiscences,* p. 20.

34 Simms, pp. 130, 132.

35 Simms, p. 128. See also Hills, pp. 1–14.

36 This valuable almanac was a gift to Rutgers by the late Harold E. Pickersgill of Perth Amboy, N.J.

37 The bourgeois (misspelled by Collins) and pica type are discussed in earlier chapters.

38 Neilson's Account Books are in the Special Collections, Rutgers University Library, part of the voluminous Neilson Papers.

39 Letter, dated January 27, 1794, in the Trenton Free Public Library.

40 Letter in Autograph Collection of Simon Gratz, HSP.

41 The receipted bill, dated July 27, 1796, is in the Trenton Free Public Library.

42 Lawrence C. Wroth, *The Colonial Printer* (Portland, 1938), p. 184.

✌ VII ✌

A FAMILY BUSINESS

1   For the letter, dated November 4, 1796, see *Reminiscences of Isaac and Rachel (Budd) Collins* (Philadelphia, 1893), pp. 58–59.

2   *Ibid.*

3   William Wade Hinshaw, *Encyclopedia of American Quaker Genealogy* (Ann Arbor, 1940), III, 80–81. See also the minutes of the Chester-field Monthly Meeting, Friends Book Store, 302 Arch Street, Philadelphia.

4   Thomas E. V. Smith, *The City of New York in the Year of Washington's Inauguration, 1789* (New York, 1889), pp. 143–144.

5   See Sidney I. Pomerantz, *New York: An American City, 1783–1803* (New York, 1938), p. 382.

6   Thomas Twining, *Travels in America 100 Years Ago* (New York, 1894), p. 152. Twining, a British official in India, visited the United States in the spring of 1796 in the course of a return trip to England.

7   See Pomerantz, pp. 199–209.

8   *The Herald; A Gazette for the Country,* September 9, 1797.

9   A. Seybert, *Statistical Annals of the U.S.* (Philadelphia, 1818), p. 142.

10 James Grant Wilson (ed.), *The Memorial History of the City of New York* (New York, 1892–1893), III, 150–151; David T. Valentine, *Manuals of the Corporation of the City of New York* (New York, 1842–1868), for the year 1855, p. 563.

11 *Archives of the State of New Jersey: Documents Relating to the Colonial History of the State of New Jersey,* ed. Frederick W. Ricord and William Nelson, First Series, XLII (1949), 91.

12 Sydney V. James, *A People Among People: Quaker Benevolence in Eighteenth-Century America* (Cambridge, Mass., 1963), p. 281.

13 *Ibid.*

14 Bliss Forbush, *Elias Hicks: Quaker Liberal* (New York, 1956), p. 113.

15 An interesting recent study is Robert W. Doherty, *The Hicksite Separation: A Sociological Analysis of Religious Schism in Early Nine-teenth-Century America* (New Brunswick, N.J., 1967).

16 Pomerantz, p. 217.
17 Harry B. Weiss, "Type Founders, Copperplate Printers, Stereotypers in Early New York City," *Bulletin of the New York Public Library,* LV (October 1951), 471–483.
18 Collins to Thomas Rotch, January 18, 1799, Rotch-Wales Papers, Friends Historical Library, Swarthmore College.
19 Quoted in Forbush, p. 92.
20 *Reminiscences,* pp. 60–61.
21 Pomerantz, p. 349.
22 *Reminiscences,* pp. 60–61.
23 *Reminiscences,* p. 50.
24 *Dictionary of National Biography* (1896 ed.), XLVI, 195–197.
25 In a letter dated January 19, 1812, to his son Joseph, *Reminiscences,* pp. 64–65.
26 Pomerantz, p. 440.
27 *The Spectator,* May 8, 1805.
28 Letter to Archibald Bartram, November 6, 1806, *Reminiscences,* p. 61.
29 The dissolution document is owned by George C. Rockefeller, Madison, N.J.
30 *Reminiscences,* p. 54.
31 Harold E. Dickson, *John Wesley Jarvis, American Painter, 1780–1840* (New York, 1949).
32 *Reminiscences,* pp. 40–41. Stephen Grellet (Etienne de Grellet du Mabillier), an evangelical leader among Quakers, was a French Catholic, educated in the Collège des Oratoriens in Lyons. He emigrated to America during the French Revolution, joined the Society of Friends in 1796, and moved to New York in 1799. He married Rebecca Collins in 1804.
33 The letter, dated November 6, 1806, is printed in *Reminiscences,* pp. 61–62.
34 *The Spectator.*
35 Rush Ms. Correspondence, Library Company of Philadelphia.
36 *Ibid.,* January 26, 1810.
37 Isaiah Thomas, *The History of Printing in America,* 2nd ed. (Albany, 1874), I, 317.
38 The letter, dated May 12, 1808, is printed in *Reminiscences,* pp. 62–63.
39 *Ibid.*
40 *Ibid.,* p. 56.
41 *New Jersey Archives,* First Series, XLII (1949), 91.
42 Two New York typefounders, John Watts and David Bruce, are both given credit for having introduced stereotyping to this country. In June 1813 Watts, whose shop was located on Broome Street near Benjamin Collins's residence, printed an edition of the *Larger Catechism of the Westminster Assembly,* claiming on the title

page that this was the first work stereotyped in America. Sometime later, Watts is believed to have sold his foundry to the Collins brothers before moving to Austria. His name disappeared from the city directory after 1815. Benjamin and Joseph Collins are said to have paid Watts $5,000 for the process. However, it is also reported that the earlier firm of Collins, Perkins & Co. was responsible for the first American stereotyping by hiring Watts, probably in 1809, the year he moved from London to New York, to make plates for an edition of Lindley Murray's *Grammar*. About 1814–15, Bruce printed several stereotyped editions of the New Testament and the Bible. See Weiss, *Bulletin of the New York Public Library*, LV, 471–483, and *Reminiscences*, p. 36n.

43 Longworth's *American Almanack, New York Register, and City Directory* for 1827 through 1838, Special Collections, Rutgers University Library; and *Reminiscences*, pp. 36–37.

44 *Reminiscences*, pp. 37–38. Mrs. Maria S. Reeve, a daughter of Richard M. and Susanna R. (Collins) Smith, wrote this impression in 1892 for the Collins family genealogy.

BIBLIOGRAPHICAL
NOTE

The basic sources for this book are cited in the notes. Here I want to single out several for special mention; some provide background and do not appear in the notes. Joseph Moxon's *Mechanick Exercises on the Whole Art of Printing,* originally published in London in 1683, is the earliest, the most complete, and the most authoritative manual available. Isaiah Thomas's two-volume *History of Printing in America,* first published in 1810, and Lawrence C. Wroth's *Colonial Printer,* issued in 1931, are still the standard guides to the printer's trade in early America. The indispensable national bibliographies of Clarence S. Brigham and Charles Evans are described in the introduction to my list of Collins imprints, as are the works of Douglas C. McMurtrie and William Nelson, who are responsible for most of what we know today about the issues of early American presses.

Basic to the biography itself is the Collins family genealogy, *Reminiscences of Isaac and Rachel (Budd) Collins,* prepared following a reunion in 1892 and published in 1893. It contains numerous letters and other accounts of some of the descendants, all of which are helpful. But, as is the case with most such affectionate studies, it serves mainly as a guide.

Collins left few personal writings, many regarding his family having been lost in a fire. The few extant letters and other items, identified in the notes, are scattered among several libraries, the richest of which are in Philadelphia and New York City. The Historical Society of Pennsylvania has Collins letters, receipts, and assorted notes in its extensive collections. The most important materials are in the Pemberton Family Papers, the Simon Gratz Autograph Collection, the Emlen Papers, and the Gardiner Collection.

Also important are the Rush Papers, Robert Aitken's Waste-Book, and the John Smith Letter Books at the Library Company of Philadelphia. The Department of Records of the Philadelphia Yearly Meeting of the Society of Friends possesses good minutes of the Burlington and Chesterfield Monthly Meetings.

In New York City the public library has custody of Collins's handwritten proposals for the *New-Jersey Gazette* and important letters in its Livingston Collection, the Flagg Papers, and the Hugh Gaine Papers. Other tangential documents are in the New-York Historical Society in the Robert Hartshorne Bowne Letter Books, the Benjamin S. Collins Receipt Books, and the Isaiah Thomas Letters.

In New Jersey Collins items are in the collections of Rutgers and Princeton university libraries. Of special value are the James Neilson Papers, the Ten Eyck Papers, and the small Collins Collection at Rutgers and the William Churchill Houston Papers, the Austin Scott Papers, and the Richard Stockton Papers at Princeton.

Other repositories for the history of the Middle States, although they do not have much original Collins material, are the American Philosophical Society, the Free Library of Philadelphia, the New Jersey State Library, the Trenton Free Public Library, the New Jersey Historical Society, the Stevens Institute (for the John Stevens Papers), the Burlington County Historical Society, Glassboro State College.

The Livingston Papers in the Massachusetts Historical Society contain several letters Collins wrote to Governor William Livingston. Rutgers has the entire collection on microfilm. Elsewhere, firsthand information relating to Collins is in the Quaker collections at Swarthmore and Haverford colleges, at Yale University, the Huntington Library, the American Antiquarian Society, the John Carter Brown Library at Brown University, the Boston Public Library, and the Historical Society of Delaware.

Contemporary newspapers are both informational and atmospheric; more than anything else, they facilitate the effort to reconstruct the old craft of the printer. Among those consulted are the *Pennsylvania Gazette,* the *Pennsylvania Chronicle,* the *Pennsylvania Packet,* and the *Pennsylvania Journal* in the Historical Society of Pennsylvania, the Library Company of Philadelphia, the American Philosophical Society, the Free Library of Philadelphia, and the American Antiquarian Society.

The New Jersey State Library in Trenton has a complete file of the *New-Jersey Gazette,* as does the New-York Historical Society. Collins presented his office file of the *Gazette,* bound in three volumes, to the society in 1815. The Trenton Free Public Library, the New Jersey Historical Society, the New York Public Library, and Rutgers and Princeton have partial files. The New York Public Library and the New-York Historical Society have outstanding files of early New York newspapers.

City directories and almanacs, in addition to being standard imprints of the early presses, provide essential data. Rutgers has one of the most complete files of directories and almanacs in existence, including all but a few years of Collins's *Burlington Almanack* and *New-Jersey Almanack.* It also has most numbers of Longworth's valuable *American Almanack, New York Register, and City Directory.*

The records of various Yearly Meetings abound with detailed and accurate information on the Society of Friends. A good starting point is William Wade Hinshaw's multivolume *Encyclopedia of American Quaker Genealogy* (Ann Arbor, Mich., 1940).

INDEX

Account Books (Franklin), 46
Account of the Convincement, Exercises, Services and Travels of Richard Davies, 21, 22
Acts of the General Assembly of The Province of New-Jersey (comp. Samuel Allison), 51, 125, 132
Adams, James, 134, 152; Collins's apprenticeship with, 6–11, 14, 18, 31
Adams, John, quoted, 63
Addison, Joseph, 20
Adventures of Telemachus (Fénelon), 35
advertising, 12, 16, 59, 127–28; by Adams, 6, 9; by Collins, 29, 31–32, 48, 74, 75, 139, 143–44, 147, 148, 150, 162, 164, 172, 173; in the *New-Jersey Gazette,* 74, 90, 122, 123, 125
Advice of Evan Ellis to His Daughter When at Sea, 9
Aesop, 125
"African trade for Negro Slaves shewn to be consistent with principles of humanity and with the laws of revealed religion, The" (Thompson), 42
Age of Reason, The (Paine), 170
agents (packetmakers), 79

agriculture, 3, 4–5, 106; barter and, 80; military needs and, 91; silk industry and, 20; texts, 172
Aitken, Robert, 44, 45–46, 79, 125; Bible of, 138, 141, 142–43
Alexander, James, 63, 108
Allinson, Samuel, 51, 83, 84, 125, 132
almanacs, 8–9, 12, 14, 29–32, 34, 35, 54, 90, 130; binding, 45; Collins's personal copy, 153
American Instructor, The (Fisher), 51
American Minerva; and Evening Advertiser, 162–63
American Philosophical Society, 15, 19, 47, 126
American Revolution, 5, 20–21, 117, 136, 161; Bible shortage in, 142–43; William Franklin and, 53–54; William Livingston and, 63, 65–66, 67, 73, 104; *New American Magazine* on, 59, 60; *New-Jersey Gazette* and, 67–69, 72–74, 81, 82, 85–93, 94, 99–100, 103–105, 110, 130, 182–83; the *Plain-Dealer* on, 61; provincial printer posts and, 34, 50–52; Rivington and, 56–57, 62; Stamp Act and, 12, 15; Townshend Act and, 16–17. *See also specific battles*

The type face used in this book is Caslon, a Linotype modification of the original design by William Caslon. The text is set in 11 point Caslon with three points of leading on a 23 pica line, and the chapter titles are set in 24 point Caslon Number 540 capitals. The book was printed by letterpress on Warren's #66 Text, basis 60 pounds, and bound in Bancroft Eton cloth. The endpapers are Multicolor Gold.